Contents

Acknowledgement

The extracts on pages 95 & 98 from *The Collected Essays, Journalism and Letters of George Orwell Volume 2, My Country Right or Left, 1940-1943* are reproduced by permission of A M Heath & Co. Ltd on behalf of Bill Hamilton as the Literary Executor of the Estate of the Late Sonia Brownell Orwell and Martin Secker & Warburg Ltd.   Copyright © George Orwell 1940-43.

Foreword

The contributors to this book represent a wide spectrum of political views and religious beliefs. It is certain that each of them disagrees with some of the views expressed here by one or more of the other contributors. Yet, despite that, they share a common *we* sentiment, a sense of Englishness that unites them.

Some are uncompromising in the way they set about making their case, others are more restrained and gentle. Whatever their approach and personality, every one of them draws strength from their Englishness, which affects their thoughts and the way they lead their lives. All have an unflinching determination to stand firm and resist those who deny the relevance or indeed the existence of an English nation. I have a high regard for every one of them and am proud to think of them as shield-companions in a small but select shieldwall.

Tony Linsell

Kathleen Herbert, a novelist and former teacher, has been an inspiration for very many people. Her passion for early English culture and the Old English language was aroused when, as a student at Oxford, she attended Tolkien's lectures. Kathleen has a vast knowledge of the period and its literature and is currently working on *The Lost Three Hundred Years* and *The Lost Tales of England*. She has kindly given permission for the reproduction here of extracts from her books, *Looking for the Lost Gods of England* and *English Heroic Legends*.

Other titles: *Queen of Lightning; Ghost in the Sunlight, Bride of the Spear; Peace-Weavers and Shield-Maidens: Women in Early English Society*.

Stephen Pollington, who works in the City of London, is a gifted linguist who has written several books, including the language course, *First Steps in Old English*. He is the long serving editor of *Widowinde*, the quarterly journal of Ða Engliscan Gesiðas (The English Companions). He has recently completed *Leechcraft: Early English Charms, Plant-Lore, and Healing*.

Other titles: *The English Warrior from earliest times to 1066; The Warrior's Way; Wordcraft: Concise English - Old English Dictionary and Thesaurus; An Introduction to the Old English Language and its Literature; Ærgeweorc: Old English Verse and Prose* (audiotape); *Rudiments of Runelore*.

Ða Engliscan Gesiðas is a non-political cultural organisation. Membership is open to anyone with an interest in early (1st millennium) English history. Details from:–
Ða Engliscan Gesiðas, BM Box 4336, London WC1N 3XX
www.kami.demon.co.uk/gesithas/index.html

Father Andrew Phillips studied Russian at Oxford and worked in Greece before studying theology in Paris. He was ordained deacon in the Orthodox Church in 1985 and priest in 1991. In 1997 he founded an Orthodox church in Felixstowe, Suffolk. He is a leading figure in the movement to attract the English to the Orthodox Church and edits the quarterly journal *Orthodox England*

Write to:– Seekings House, Garfield Road, Felixstowe, Suffolk IP11 7PU

Other titles: *Orthodox Christianity and the Old English Church; The Hallowing of England; The Rebirth of England and English: The Vision of William Barnes; Orthodox Christianity and the English Tradition; The Lighted Way; The Story of St Felix.*

Tony Linsell is a publisher and a founding member of the Campaign for an English Parliament. His contribution to this book is an extract from *An English Nationalism,* which is to be published Spring 2000.

The Campaign for an English Parliament is a cross-party organisation that unites people of diverse political views around the aim of obtaining a parliament for England. Campaign for an English Parliament, 1 Providence Street, King's Lynn, Norfolk PE30 5ET

www.englishpm.demon.co.uk

Rev. John Lovejoy has spent many years in various parts of the world observing people and cultures. In his contribution to this collection, *The Paradox,* he mentions a paper he sent to the Home Office in 1986. That paper has recently been published as *The Deculturalisation of the English People.*

Geoffrey Littlejohns has spent many years researching the history of English radicalism. He has written several articles on the subject and has a particular interest in John Lilburne and The Levellers. He served as Secretary of Ða Engliscan Gesiðas for many years and has played an important part in that organisation's success.

Gárman Lord is an English-American with a consuming interest in the pre-Christian indigenous communal values and perceptions of the English, which he is intent on formulating and promoting. He is a founder and the leader of Theod, a group that has, since 1975, been piecing together and practising an Anglo-Saxon heathenry.

Theod, PO Box 8062, Watertown, New York 13601, USA

Other titles: *The Way of the Heathen* and
To be or not to be: The Plight of the English-American, to be published Spring 2000.

The Early English

Kathleen Herbert

The first thing to bear in mind is that the country now called England is, in fact, our second England, New England. The first England – Old Anglia, Engla land, Angeln – was in the south of the country we now call Denmark. Angeln was in the narrow neck of the Cimbric peninsula, with the River Eider as its southern frontier. This frontier was defended and fixed by King Offa I, in one of the great exploits of early English tradition, a tale of self-penalising honour that is very nearly a thousand years older than the medieval Age of Chivalry.

Therefore, during our formative period of at least two thousand years, the centre of our world was a good way further to the east, so our world-view was very different from that of today.

The world, as the early Germans knew it, offered vast scope for adventure and rich food for the imagination, from the wastes of Lappland to the dazzling splendours of Constantinople and Rome; from the eastern steppes, where the Gothic horsemen came up against the Iranian Sarmatians and Alans and the Turkic Huns, to the western "country-house" life in the villas of Gaul and Spain.

The English did not leave that world behind when they crossed the sea and founded their new England. They brought their stories with them and went on re-creating them in their poetry. Only a fragment of Old English poetry remains: one epic only survives as two scraps that were later used in book-binding.

English poets and their listeners seem to have been stirred most (judging by the remaining material; but surviving by luck and chance, this may not be completely representative) by the stories which had grown up around their own Baltic and North Sea coasts: Offa 's defence of the English border and his winning of a perilous maiden; the self-destruction of the Scylding House; the exploits of Beowulf; Hengest's bitter choices; the agony of Weland; the doomed enchantment of Heoden's love for Hild.

The English were a Baltic people. The Romans said that they had remained undisturbed and inaccessible by enemies *"fluminibus aut silvüs muniuntur"*, fortified with rivers and forests.[1] Archaeology confirms that there was no invasion of peoples or cultures from the outside, during a period from the beginning of the Northern Bronze Age (c. 1500 BCE) to the Migrations of the third century CE onwards.

This means that the people who called themselves *Engle* (written as *Anglii* in Latin) were forming their group-identity during the brilliant Bronze Age culture of the Cimbric peninsula, that has left such spectacular and mind-teasing remains: the curved

---

[1] *Germania* ch. 40.

ceremonial trumpets, the *lurs*; the ritual horned helmets; the fine metal-work of weapons, collars and drinking-horns; the figurines of girls in the briefest of cord mini-skirts (they really did wear them; the garments have been found in burials); above all, the carved rock-pictures.[2]

These images seem to be concerned with evoking and celebrating fertility. Such images have been used worldwide for this purpose: the tree; the horned animal; the man with the erect penis; the pairing of man and woman; the acrobatic leaps that symbolise energy and growth. Particularly significant in relation to later English practices are the *ship*, slim and light in build; the *waggon* or *wain*; the *plough* and above all the *sun*, represented as a disc with crossing spokes, which is often being used as a *shield* by the stick-like male figures.

In Old English and other Germanic languages the sun is feminine: in the north, she is gentle, life-giving, nurturing; she does not burn the earth or strike folk to death.

The earliest surviving mention of the English as a separate tribe comes in the *Germania* of Tacitus, published in 98 CE. Tacitus describes German society of the first century as being of the 'heroic' type, which existed at different periods, and with regional variations, among the Indo-European peoples from India to Ireland. The leading characters in these societies are the kings and chiefs and their 'companions', élite warriors bound to their lords by ties of honour, courage and generosity.

Tacitus mentions three great gods by more or less equivalent Latin names: Mars, Mercury and Hercules; later the Romans corrected the last name to Jupiter. These gods were known in Old English as Tiw, Woden and Thunor, who are still commemorated in the weekday names Tuesday *Tīwes dæg*, Wednesday *Wōdnes dæg* and Thursday *Þunres dæg*. When English scholars learned to read and write in Latin, they accepted these Roman names as reasonably accurate translations. Tacitus stresses that the Germans believed there was something specially holy about woman as a sex, "*sanctum aliquid*"[3]; that they had special prophetic powers; that men consulted them and followed their advice on matters of politics and war.

The English seem to have conformed to the general Germanic pattern, because Tacitus says that there was nothing noteworthy about them and the six tribes who shared in their worship *except one thing*. However, he found that one exception so interesting and important that he gave it a whole chapter in a very short book:

> They worship in common Nerthus, that is Terra Mater [Earth Mother] and believe she intervenes in human affairs and goes on progress through the

---

[2] For the rock-pictures see the *Chariot of the Sun*, P. Gelling with H. E. Davidson, 1969.

For pre-historic Denmark see *Land of the Tollund Man*, P. Lauring trans. R. Spink, 1957

There is a good selection of illustrations in *Scandinavian Mythology*, H. E. Davidson, 1982 but the reader must note the place and date of the finds to see which material is relevant to the Anglii and their allies.

[3] *Germania* ch. 8.

tribes. There is a sacred grove on an island of the ocean, and in the grove is a consecrated waggon [or wain] covered with a cloth [possibly embroidered or woven with golden thread, like the scraps found in the Taplow burial]. Only one priest is allowed to touch it; he understands when the goddess is present in her shrine and follows with profound reverence when she is drawn away by cows [*bubus feminis*]. Then there are days of rejoicing: the places she considers worthy to entertain her– [that is, wherever the cows drawing the wain, which has no human driver, come to a stop] –keep holiday. They do not go to war, do not use weapons, all iron is shut away – peace and quiet are so much esteemed and loved at that time – until the same priest returns the goddess to her sanctuary when she has had enough of human company. Directly, the wain, the covering cloth and, if you like to believe this, [here Tacitus, the sophisticated Roman, distances himself from the English and their primitive beliefs] the goddess herself, are washed in a secluded lake. Slaves are the ministers; immediately, the same lake swallows them. [They are drowned as soon as they have finished their task; lay folk may not see or touch the goddess and live.] From this arises a mysterious terror and a pious ignorance about what that may be, which is only seen by those about to die.[4]

So, the noteworthy characteristic of the English, to foreign eyes, was that they were goddess-worshippers; they looked on the earth as their mother.

They did not leave this relationship behind them when they crossed over to another part of the earth; not even when they had crossed over to another state religion. Among the Old English healers' prescriptions, which in their surviving forms were written down in the tenth and eleventh centuries, is one named *Æcerbot*: Field-Remedy.[5] It is called a 'charm'; in fact, it is a full-scale ritual which would take a whole day to perform, as well as the time needed to collect and prepare all the materials that it calls for.

As we have it, the ritual has been extensively Christianised. It not only entails much reciting of Latin liturgical texts by the healer, but it needs four masses, to be said over four turfs that are taken to church and placed with their grassy sides facing the altar. These turfs represent the sick field. This could only happen with the approval and co-operation of the parish priest. Four masses could take up most of a morning; there is no way that the priest could be unaware – or even pretend to be unaware – what was going on. And what was going on, after her healing, was a mating of Mother Earth with the God of Heaven and her impregnation by Him.

---

[4] *Germania* ch. 40.
[5] See Rodrigues and Cockayne, works cited in footnote 2 above. There is a translation in *Anglo-Saxon Poetry*, S. A. J. Bradley, 1982.

Leaving out the recitation of Latin texts, what happened was this: Mother Earth, in this particular field, was weak and sick, unable to bear. Perhaps she had been deliberately injured by hostile magic.

The healer cut a turf from each of the four quarters: east, south, west and north, noting carefully exactly where each had lain. These turfs for the time being represented – *were* the whole field. A mixture was made of vegetable matter from every tree and shrub that grew locally, except hardwoods, and all known herbs except buckbean. These were blended with oil, honey, holy water and milk from all the cattle on the farm. This mixture was dropped three times on the underside of the turfs.

Mother Earth was being given healing herbs, mixed with a nourishing porridge to strengthen her.

Then the turfs went to church for their four masses. Presumably these replaced something that was once done in a temple or a sacred grove. They were put back exactly where they came from, but first, four crosses made of 'quickbeam' – the name was used later for both the rowan and the wild service tree – with the names of the evangelists cut on their ends, were placed in the earth under them.

In the light of what follows, these crosses may originally have been the spokes of the sun-wheel, with *sigel* ᛚ and other appropriate runes cut in them, but this is only guess-work.

The healer faced eastwards, praying to "*þone haligan heofonrices weard ... and heofones meaht and heah reced,*" the holy guardian of the heavenly kingdom ... and the might of heaven and the high hall; then turned three times with the course of the sun and fell prostrate on the earth.

The warmth and life-giving power of the sun was now pouring down through the body of the healer on to and into Mother Earth.

Then the plough was got ready. A hole was drilled into the plough beam and another mixture was put into it: incense, fennel and consecrated salt, blended with consecrated salve. (*Sape* means 'salve', 'unguent', or 'soap' in Old English.) Had the priest blessed the ointment, whatever it was – or did he let them use the oil for anointing the sick?

After the anointing, seed specially bought from beggars at double the value was placed on the body of the plough. The plough, which figures in the Bronze Age rock pictures, is a traditional symbol for the penis. Shakespeare describes Cleopatra's seduction of Julius Caesar as:

> She made great Caesar lay his sword to bed,
> ˙ he ploughed her and she cropped...

which is exactly what this ritual was designed to bring about. Before the plough/penis was put into Mother Earth, it had to be anointed and made potent with semen.

The healer then recited a prayer that the earth might be granted a bountiful harvest and be kept safe from all harm "from witchcrafts (or poisons) sown across the land". The opening line of this prayer is mysterious: "*Erce, erce, erce, eorþan modor* –Erce, erce, erce, Mother of Earth", with its three-fold and untranslated invocation and the fact that the power being addressed is not Mother Earth but the Mother of Earth, whoever she may be.

Then the plough was set in motion and the first furrow was cut as the marriage-blessing was recited:

> Hal wes þu, folde, fira modor,
> beo þu growende on Godes fæðme,
> fodre gefylled firum to nytte

> Hail to you, earth, mother of mortals, may you grow big in God's embrace,
> filled with food for the use of humankind.

Mother Earth was being penetrated and impregnated, but one wonders which god was supposed to be doing it. At the time this ritual was written down, the official answer should have been Jehovah, but this is not easy to visualise.

Then the healer, or the assistants, took flour made from every kind of grain, kneaded with milk and holy water. A loaf or cake was baked, as big as would fit into a pair of hollowed palms, and put inside the first furrow with another blessing. Mother Earth has got a corn-baby.

So, as the count of years was adding up to 1,000 of the Christian era, the English were still in the service of Nerthus. They went on serving her through all the upheavals of history for the next thousand years.

Alone at Monster–Gate

Kathleen Herbert

In the old days, Wærmund son of Wihtlæg, Woden-born, was ruling in Angeln. This was before the Angelcynn went away overseas to the west.

Wærmund was a very great man. He was so great in size and strength that he seemed to be giant-born as well as god-born. He was even greater in courage, truth and generosity. The farming-folk obeyed him because he gave them fair dealing and kept them safe from raiders. His warriors were devoted to him because he led them to victory and plunder. The scops who made poems about him said that his gold-hoard was as vast as a mountain and his gifts flowed out of it like a river. He was a good king.

He had ruled for a long time; he had three surviving sons come to manhood. All these princes had inherited a good share of their father's strength and spirit. Luckily, they seemed to be good friends. The eldest showed no distrust of his brothers; the younger ones showed no envy. The eldest was lately married to a Jutish princess. Soon there would be grandchildren to carry on the royal line.

So Wærmund had good cause to be proud and happy. When he looked ahead, as a wise man must, to his coming old age and death, he was content to think of his sons guarding and guiding the Angelcynn in his place. Life had done well by him and he had done well with his life.

But Wyrd goes ever as she must. A life cannot be judged till it is over. Wærmund had many more years of kingship to endure before stronger hands took it from him.

His eldest son was killed horse-breaking before he had got his young wife with child. The second son dutifully took his brother's place and his widow. He was killed the same year, fighting off a Myrging raid in the southern borderlands. Then a wet summer, a ruined harvest and a bitter winter brought hunger and weakness to the farm-folk.

When the raiding season was over, and folk were keeping Mothers' Night at the dark heart of midwinter, the Myrgings attacked again. They struck at Angeln in mockery and contempt, to show that they could do as they liked on English land. They did not win much loot – there was not much to be had that year – but they came, they burned and they went home again without being stopped or punished. They boasted about it. Other tribes took note.

The Jutish king sent for his twice-widowed sister to come home before she could be married to her second brother-in-law. He thought that Wyrd had turned against the English. They were marked out for bad luck and he wanted no share of it.

When the warm weather came, fever came with it. Many folk died. Wærmund lost his last son and also his queen, his wise and faithful companion. He was alone, an ageing, childless king. There were too many nobles in Angeln linked to the royal house by marriage and descent, all ready to start a civil war as soon as he died or lost control of his war-band.

He sent envoys with precious gifts to his neighbour, the king of the Wærnas. The embassy came back with the king's daughter, a quiet, gracious girl. She was proud to be King Wærmund's bride; she truly wished to be a good queen to the English. She offered many sacrifices and gave rich gifts to the gods. She prayed that she might bear a prince who would be as great a man as his father.

It looked as if the gods had granted her prayer. She was soon with child; she grew so great and heavy that her every move was a struggle. Her women whispered among themselves. They were afraid the king's enemies had hired a sorcerer to cast runes against the queen's childbearing, to make her litter a dozen tiny creatures at one birth, all too weak to draw breath. When her time came, though, it was clear that she was carrying one child, so big that it could only force its way out into the light after a long struggle.

The queen bore her terrible labour with great courage. She would not let herself scream aloud, bringing her child to birth to the sounds of pain and fear. She made her women sing ballads about the deeds of gods and heroes; she joined in the singing while she could. Near the end, she could only moan and gasp for breath, but she kept as quiet as possible.

Her courage – and her prayers and gifts to the gods – seemed to be rewarded. She gave the English a prince, a big healthy boy, strong and likely to thrive. She did not enjoy her triumph and the king's gratitude for long. She had given too much of herself to her son's making, flesh, blood and spirit. What was left of her life flickered for a little while, then went out.

Care for his last child first taught Wærmund to dread death. He had no wish to marry again. His heir must have no half-brothers to envy him, to be used as gaming pieces against him by nobles greedy for power. The king felt very old; he told himself grimly that he must try to stay alive and hold the land until Prince Offa had grown to manhood, able to handle weapons and rule warriors.

Meanwhile, though, Prince Offa belonged with his wet-nurses. He must be placed under the care of some high-born lady, the ruler of a great household, who knew how to guard a child's well-being.

Luckily, Wærmund's most powerful kinsman was the one he trusted and liked best, with good reason. Earl Freawine held the southern march against the Myrgings. They were troublesome folk to have over the border, restless and defiant. They were not a large or powerful tribe but they had the mighty nation of the Swabians at their back. The Myrgings were an off-shoot of the Swabians; they claimed the high-king as their lord and protector when it suited them. Most of the time, though, they did as they liked.

Freawine was a stern lord, unbroken in battle, rock-like in faith. He would make a good foster-father for the prince, to teach him warriors' honour and sword-play. His wife was well-born and wise. Also, he had two lusty sons, Wigheard and Cedd, just growing up to manhood. They would be guards, play-fellows and, later, brothers-in-arms to their prince.

So Offa, his nurses and servants were sent south with rich gifts for Earl Freawine and his lady.

Offa was well cared-for in his new home and grew at a great rate. His appetite was as big as everything else about him; he sucked like a young bull-calf. He was a good baby in that he hardly ever cried – but he hardly ever laughed either. His nurses claimed that he knew his mother had died to give him life. When he was awake, he stared hard at the world around him. He pushed and kicked out lustily whenever he was unwrapped from his swaddling-clouts. His body was flawless; every woman in the household doted on him. Yet weeks, months, a year passed, then two, and still he had not started to babble, however much his nurses coaxed him to talk.

When he first arrived, Wigheard and Cedd had come to their mother's bower to look at him. They had dangled their arm-rings and jewelled belt-buckles within reach of his fingers. They got no response but a solemn wide-eyed stare. They decided he was feeble-minded.

'He's an old man's get,' said Wigheard, a worldly-wise man of fourteen. 'They're always lacking somewhere – body, brain or heart.'

His mother cried out in protest.

'Offa's not stupid – look at his eyes! He's taking in everything we do and say. He'll talk when he's ready.'

'He'll be none the worse if he grows up to think before he speaks,' said Earl Freawine. 'That's a lesson you'd do well to learn, young Wiga.'

Freawine's sons had mixed feelings about having the young prince in their household. They were proud that the king had singled out their family for the trust. Wigheard was old enough to see that their father was now second man in the kingdom. He would be first man if Wærmund died before Offa was fit to rule.

Wigheard had already decided that Offa would never be fit to rule. He looked ahead twelve years, when Offa would be a man. By then, Wærmund would surely be dead and Freawine would be old.

Wigheard had no doubt that he would be the next king. His grandmother had been old King Wihtlæg's sister. He was too proud to harbour any thought that seemed like planned treachery. He told himself that idiots cannot rule. Angeln would need a strong-minded, warlike king.

Cedd was two years younger than his brother. His life was driven by two powerful forces: his hero-worship of Wiga and a burning wish to match him, if not out-do him. He followed Wiga zestfully into every scrape.

Both youths were ready to swagger around the tun as Prince Offa's picked champions. They were unwilling to give up any of their own amusements for his sake. When their father told them to stay at home from the first great hunting party of autumn and keep guard over the prince, they would have rebelled if they dared. Cedd could only curse over his lost sport; Wiga had other ideas how to pass their time pleasantly.

He had lately bought a Hunnish bow from a passing trader. That strange half-demon race was supreme in archery. Their bows were cunningly-made of horn, wood and sinew, with a double curve above and below the grip, so that though they seemed short, they had a longer draw and a much greater force than self bows. But Hunnish bows need skilled handling. Wiga did not want to make his first attempts with it in public, for the household to jeer at. He told Cedd they would go and practise on the water-fowl down by the river. There was no fear that their father would see or hear of them; he had ridden off to the heath-lands.

'He'll hear we flouted his orders. He told us we weren't to leave Offa.'

'We won't leave him. We'll take him with us.'

'You're mad.'

'He'll be no trouble. He always sleeps like a log after his morning feed.'

'His nurse won't let us take him out.'

'Eanswið always sleeps like a log too, after she's fed him. We'll get the maid to bring him out under her cloak.'

'She wouldn't dare.'

'She will if I tell her to. I can make Leofrun do anything I want.'

Wiga stuck his thumbs in his belt and straddled his legs, grinning.

Leofrun was scared but did as she was told. They made their way out of the tun, unseen, through the herb-patch and the orchard. They were soon hidden in the skirts of the forest.

The woods sloped down towards the river-bank. The land there was sour and marshy, unfit for crops or cattle. They did not expect to meet anyone. Then their path came out into a patch of open ground, where a man was at work.

He was undoing the carcass of a boar; its head was already off. Nearby stood a foundered horse, its head drooping. The man heard a twig crack; he looked round, then got to his feet, gripping his bloody hand-seax. Wiga and Cedd stood watching him. Leofrun drew back among the bushes, clutching Offa.

The stranger was a tall, powerfully-built man, dressed in plain workmanlike clothes of leather and dark wool. A knowing eye would have seen that his gear and his horse were of good quality. Young Wiga still judged a man's rank by his jewellery and embroidered borders, so he thought this one must be a churl. He noted that the stranger's hair was drawn back and knotted on the crown of his head, in the fashion of the Swabians, also their allies and hangers-on. Worst of all, however tall Wiga drew himself up, the stranger could look down on him. Wiga lost his temper.

'You Myrgings are stupid. You can't remember which side of the river you live on. I'll have to teach you another lesson.'

The stranger looked more amused than angry.

'You should have explained that to the boar when he crossed the water. I expect you can talk boarish. It's too late to argue with him now. As for me, no quarry of mine can go where I don't follow.'

The Myrging laughed, but pleasantly enough, so that his words could be taken as a joke rather than a challenge if his listeners chose. He was alone, not taking part in a raid. He had simply been unwilling to lose his quarry, a feeling that any hunter could share. Also, he had tackled it single-handed, so he must be brave as well as skilful.

An older man, more sure of himself, would have decided to take the words as a joke, joined in the laugh, perhaps invited the hunter home with him for food and rest before he crossed the river again.

Wiga had only just taken arms; he was not as sure of himself as he made out. He thought the Myrging was sneering at him in front of his younger brother and his girl.

'That's why you're going to end like your quarry, in the same place!' He drew his sword.

The hunter looked down on him with some kindliness for his pluck.

'Go home, pup. I don't want to hurt you. Fighting's for warriors. Run along and play with the other children.'

He glanced at Cedd, Leofrun and baby Offa, clearly putting Wigheard with them. Wiga nearly choked with fury.

'Yes, fighting is for warriors. Weaklings are only big-mouthed. Fight me if you dare. Dare or not, I'm going to kill you for treading on my land.'

Cedd moved closer to his brother, ready to keep his side and back. The hunter shifted his seax to his left hand and drew his sword.

'If that's your choice, you'd better come on together, for both your sakes. I'm more than a match for the pair of you.'

'No! Stay where you are, Cedd. Don't you dare interfere. I claim single combat. He's mine!'

He hurled himself at the Myrging.

At first, it was clear that the hunter meant to play with him for a while, then disarm him – maybe give him a drubbing on the backside with the flat of his sword to teach him not to pester his elders.

It is not easy to play with a strong, agile youngster, killing-mad and armed with a good sword. In a few seconds the Myrging was fighting in earnest. His strength and reach, his greater skill and experience gave him the mastery. Wigheard knew he had met his master; he was hitting out in mindless rage, then tripped and fell heavily, dropping his sword. If the Myrging had not paused in mid-stroke, he could have skewered him.

Cedd watched in anguish, torn apart by shame and honour. By refusing the stranger's offer to fight both at once, by claiming single combat, Wigheard had made it impossible for Cedd to join in on his brother's side. The Myrging had no fear that he would; more than once he had turned his back on Cedd, in perfect faith that Cedd would not lift a hand against him. No warrior could do so; he would kill his own honour with the first blow.

So he must just stand there, watch his brother being killed and do nothing? What sort of honour was that?

Anyway, when Wiga was dead, he would have to challenge the Myrging, to avenge his brother. He'd be killed too – if Wiga couldn't beat him, nobody could. And then, what would become of Offa?

If the Myrging wasn't blood-drunk enough to kill him and Leofrun at once – if Leofrun had time to say who the child was – what a trophy he would be for the Myrgings to gloat over, while they decided whether to sell him to a trader, keep him as a thrall, or make Wærmund humble himself begging them to take ransom.

Father and mother would be disgraced for ever – left to face Wærmund's fury with no sons to protect them –

Father had ordered them to guard Offa above all things – surely he'd want them to do anything, however dreadful –

– *Anyway, I haven't taken sword yet – I'm not a warrior – I'm not bound by* –

Wiga was on his feet again, breathless and unsteady but still refusing to yield. He threw himself at his enemy like a madman. Once again, his blows were parried, his sword knocked from his hand, he was beaten to the ground. The Myrging was angry now. He kicked Wiga's sword out of his reach and stooped over him.

'Go to Hel, then, if that's what you want – I wish Her joy of you.'

Before he could strike the death-blow, Cedd's hand-seax went into his back with all the force of Cedd's arm behind it. He crashed down spewing blood, twitched and was still.

Wigheard slowly got up. Neither brother spoke; they both knew what had happened was unspeakable. Wiga took his own seax; he went behind a thicket of alders and began cutting turfs. Cedd joined him. When they had cleared enough ground, they hollowed out a grave.

Luckily, the Myrging had fallen forwards; they did not have to look him in the face. They spread his cloak alongside him, rolled him onto it and wrapped it tightly around him. They carried him to the grave and laid him out in it as decently as they could, with his hunting spear, his sword and his seax beside him. They piled the earth over him and laid the turfs, stamping them down and scattering fallen leaves over them.

They dealt with the boar more briefly by dragging it a good way in the opposite direction and leaving it where the undergrowth was thickest. There would only be scattered bones left of it by morning.

They did not want another tell-tale corpse to hide, so they dragged and beat the horse down to the river and stoned it away from the bank. The current was strong; the wretched beast was swept a good way downstream before it started trying to swim.

When they got back to the glade among the alders, Leofrun was still standing like a tree-stump. She stared at them. Her cloak had fallen open. Offa was awake now, he was sitting up in her arms. He stared at them too.

Cedd hated the girl for having watched them.

'Best cut her throat and bury her too. We'll say she ran off to amuse herself and left the child.'

'Leofrun won't talk.' Wiga smiled at her terrified face. 'She's a good girl. She'll say no more about it than *he* will.'

He jerked his thumb at Offa.

'Can we be sure he won't tell when he starts to talk? Remember how mother said he takes in everything we do –'

'I don't believe that. He just gapes like an idiot. Even if he should talk about it – if he ever talks! – we'll just talk him down. We'll say he must have had a dream about a story Leofrun told to amuse him.'

Long before they came home, they had been missed and searched for. Wiga boldly outfaced the resentment of the guards, the outcry from Eanswið the nurse, the anger of his mother.

Father had told them not to leave Offa; they hadn't left Offa for a single minute. They had taken him to watch them trying the Hunnish bow, as a treat. They thought it would be good for him to see men's pastimes instead of spending the whole day with women. Wiga's clothes were bloody and torn because he had gone up a tree after a wild cat and had fallen off a branch when it sprang at him. No he wasn't hurt, only a few scratches. They had been doing their best; they thought folk would be pleased with them. All right, they promised not to do anything like it again.

They kept their word.

When winter was over and traders could travel again, they brought a strange story across the Eider. The Myrgings had lost their king, Eadgils. He had out-ridden his hunting companions, going after a huge boar that had killed his hounds and two of his men before breaking out of the ring that was baying him. Eadgils often boasted that he never let a quarry escape him, however far he had to follow it or what wild land he had to cross. Not one of his men was surprised that he had not come back by sunset. They only began to search on the second day. They never saw their king again.

A while later, a Myrging fisherman had found what was left of a drowned horse in the mud, far down towards Eidermouth. It had fine trappings; the fisher took them to his chief, who recognised the designs on the metal-work. Perhaps the king had been lured to his death by a water-demon that had taken the shape of a boar to bring him into the river and drown him. The Eider was known as 'Fifel-dor', the Monster-Gate, because of the otherworld horrors that swam inland from the ocean with the sea-fogs and the raging winter gales.

Some of the Myrgings were inclined to blame the English for the loss of their king. That was because they blamed the English for most of their troubles. They had no idea that Eadgils had crossed into Angeln; they suspected he had caught an English raiding party on his borderland and attacked them single-handed. Yet no Myrging had seen or suffered from raiders. No word came out of Angeln boasting of a king-slaying.

No word about Eadgils' death came from Angeln because no such word was spoken. Leofrun kept her mouth shut. She got a brooch from Wiga; also, next summer, a baby. Offa never spoke a word about what he had seen, through all the years of his childhood, because he never spoke at all. The king's only son was a dumb idiot.

Freawine's household shut their minds to the fact as long as they could. The lady still insisted that Offa understood everything that was said and done around him. Eanswið and the other womenservants told each other about children they knew who had not said a word till they were three years old – or even four – then talked all the better when they did begin. No one knew a story about a child who had not spoken till he was five – six – seven, half way to manhood. No one had ever heard Offa speak one human word. After he stopped making baby-noises, his silence was unbroken.

They gathered healing herbs at the due times with many incantations; they brewed potions for him to drink and made salves to rub on his throat. They said charms over him, engraved loosening runes on amulets to hang round his neck, offered sacrifices and gave treasures to the gods. Nothing they did could win or buy a voice for Offa.

Earl Freawine and his lady grieved for their king and for the boy. He was the image of a prince, tall and strong as a young Thunor, with handsome features and clear grey eyes. He had always been active and healthy; he could swim like a fish, even when the Eider was ice-cold and swollen with melted snow. He followed every hunt – only chaining would have kept him at home – running tirelessly beside Freawine's horse. He must have had some animal sense, he was good at tracking and turning game; he seemed fearless. In the tun, he squatted patiently for hours, watching the young warriors at their weapon-play. He would have made a fine hound.

For some years there was little trouble from the Myrgings. Eadgils had left sons; the eldest was old enough and fit to rule but there were uncles and cousins who thought themselves fitter. There was civil war, with a savage kinslaying among the nobles of royal blood.

Wærmund was glad of the respite. If he had been younger, he would have been raiding beyond the Eider and taking tribute from the Myrgings. Angeln seemed as strong as ever, but only because it had not been attacked; it could no longer make its power felt beyond its borders.

The king was still respected by most of his own folk. He believed that his counsellors and his war-band would be faithful, even at a last stand. But there was no longer the old intense rivalry to join his household. Foreign champions did not offer their services to him now. The younger English nobles were going away to other lands, to serve more warlike kings who offered the chance of winning honour and plunder. He heard of some who were with the Jutes, the Danes, the Frisians, the Franks. He guessed by what he did not hear about some others that they had gone to the Swabians.

The glory of Angeln was fading into twilight. Darkness was coming even sooner on Wærmund. His eyes were failing. Offa was now nearly fourteen, young to be a king but old enough, if he had good counsel. He sent for his heir.

Freawine had warned the king long ago that Offa was sluggish and unwilling to put himself forward. Pity had kept him from telling the father just how backward his son was. Also, he had kept hoping that some sorcerer would find a cure for the dumbness or that the gods would give the boy a voice.

So, wishing the king nothing but well, Freawine made the death of his hope more painful when it came. If Offa had been feeble or deformed, the sense of loss would have been less bitter. He looked all that an æðeling should be. At the first meeting, it seemed to Wærmund's fading eyes that his long-dead eldest son had come back from his grave-mound to help his father in the hour of need.

Then the old king learned that this last son was a mute. He took the blow as bravely as he had borne all the others that life had dealt him. He settled Offa quietly in a hall of his own inside the royal tun, with a guard of trusted old warriors. Eanswið, who was devoted to him, kept the house.

Wærmund could not stop folk talking. Soon, gloating voices across the Myrging border were spreading the tale that the English æðeling was a drooling idiot, a man of fourteen still in the keeping of his wet-nurse. He knew that the Myrgings would attack soon.

The Myrgings now had a stronger power to back them. In exchange for help in wiping out his kin, the new chief, Meaca, had taken King Witta of the Swabians as his overlord. The Myrgings no longer had a kingdom; Meaca was holding the land for King Witta and took his orders. He paid tribute; his younger brother Mearcweard was a hostage among the Swabians, serving in the king's war-band.

Meaca was willing to pay this price for being chief man among his own people and for the hope of bringing Angeln down. King Witta's eyes were looking north; he had picked Angeln as his next prey, with the Myrgings as his hunting-hounds.

Wærmund told his council that a blind man could not rule. Freawine would be the next king, with Wigheard as his heir. In return for the kingship, Freawine must adopt Offa as his son and promise to protect him.

At midwinter, the Myrgings tried another surprise attack, not a raid this time; they struck with all their force. Freawine was ready for them and brought them to a standstill when they had only got a little way north of the Eider. But he was slain, with Cedd at his side. Wigheard, fighting with the battle-fury of Woden, rallied his men, broke the Myrging host and drove them headlong back through the river. Two days later he died of his wounds.

Meaca called on his overlord to protect the Myrgings against further English attacks and make them pay wergild for the blood they had shed. King Witta promised his help.

Wærmund told the boy who guided his steps to lead him to the war-chest, take out a sword and put the hilt in his hand. He tried two or three for weight, balance and ease of grip, found one to his liking and sheathed it in his empty scabbard. The boy was puzzled but said nothing. No one questioned Wærmund's actions, even when he was old and blind.

When he first knew that he was losing his sight, Wærmund had taken his own sword and gone out alone from the royal tun. The sword was Weland's work; it was precious, not so much for the wrought gold and garnets that gleamed on its hilt but for its strength and cutting edge. Its name was Stedefæst, because it could be trusted to cut through anything in its way, however hard, at a single blow.

Wærmund had made up his mind that King Witta would never lay hands on Stedefæst as a prize of war, to boast about in his own tun or, worse, give away as a reward to his Myrging henchmen.

He went far out to the desolate moorland, to one of the grave-mounds of the ancient kings, so long dead that even the scops did not know their names. Hawthorns covered the hill-side. The barrow was girdled with nettles, brambles grew thickly all over it but the huge stones at the entrance could still be seen.

He could not open the mound by himself. He walked east from the portal till he came to an old thorn tree and buried his sword at its foot. Then he went back, counting his paces, to the stone blocking the entrance to the barrow. Lifting the bramble-fronds aside, he scratched ↑ with his seax – the sign of Tiw, the bravest and most faithful of the gods, who had sacrificed his sword-hand to keep his word. Underneath, he cut the thorn rune þ and a mark for each pace. So he left Stedefæst under the protection of the Sword God. Any weapon from the war-chest would do for his last stand, when the Swabians came across the Eider.

The first Swabians to cross the Eider carried green branches. They called themselves envoys, coming in peace and offering friendship. Their manners were insolent. They swaggered into the king's hall like conquerors. Their spokesman was Mearcweard the Myrging. He was widely known and feared for his swordsmanship. He often said that no living man had fought with him; it was his favourite joke.

'King Witta is merciful. He'll let you spend the rest of your days as chief, if you take him as overlord and pay tribute. Your folk can go on living in Angeln to farm the land. Also, you must swear never to lift a hand against his kinsmen, the Myrgings. You must give us all the land up to ten miles north of the Eider, to keep our borders safe from your thieving. And you must pay us whatever wergild we set for our blood you have shed.'

He grinned at the scowling faces of Wærmund's men.

'If you don't like the terms, send a champion of royal blood to meet me by the Eider this day week and settle the matter once and for all. The king will be on the southern bank by then with his warriors. He'll expect an answer – fight or yield. What do you say?'

Wærmund waited inside his darkness, listening.

In the old days, the hall would have been shaking to the roar of warriors trying to shout each other down, all claiming the right to take up the challenge.

No one spoke.

Wærmund's men were loyal, willing to die with their king. But for too long, their thoughts had been fixed on a hopeless last stand. Their spirits were not ready to challenge Wyrd at a moment's notice.

The silence only lasted a moment, long enough to bring Wærmund's heart near to breaking. Slowly, he got to his feet. He spoke out into the darkness towards the jeering voice.

'All my life I've led my people. My strength has ebbed and my eyes are dark, but I am still the king. I only fight my equals. Tell King Witta I'll meet him in combat, if he'll stand to exchange blows with me.'

Mearcweard guffawed; his companions joined in the laugh.

'You're in your dotage! King Witta wouldn't stoop to strike you. Even if you could see what you're doing, there isn't enough blood in your carcass to redden his sword-blade. You've wasted enough of my time. You've heard your orders. Obey them.'

Without the courtesy of leavetaking, he turned to go.

'Not so fast, Myrging. You haven't got our answer to take back to your master.'

Mearcweard stopped abruptly, glaring round for the speaker. He did not like the sound of 'your master'.

The words had come from a broad-shouldered man sitting near the door. He was well-dressed but his lowly place showed he was not of much account. Also, he was very young; he could barely have finished his weapon-training. He was likely showing-off in front of the older men, trusting that no foreign warrior would take a challenge from him and that his own folk would never let such a raw lad step forward in their name.

The youngster spoke again. His voice was level and slow, as if he thought of each word on its own before he said it.

'Tell your king to gather his tribute somewhere else, unless he wants it in spears, or a sword through his guts. That's all he – or you – will ever get from Angeln.'

Mearcweard sneered. 'Lip-courage! Stop yapping at my heels or you'll get kicked. You know very well I'd never agree to meet you in single combat.'

'Don't be afraid. I'm not asking you to meet me in single combat. I want a fair fight, so I'll let you bring a friend.'

Mearcweard nearly choked on the insult. A few seconds passed before he could answer.

'Very well, you young whelp. You'll get what you've asked for.'

The envoys left. No one else moved or spoke.

Then Wærmund said, 'Who answered for Angeln?'

The household was almost dumbstruck. He heard someone clear his throat and mutter, ' Your son, lord.'

'Don't mock me. Whoever he is, he spoke like an æðeling and he shall have an æðeling's place. Let him come to the high table.'

Heavy footsteps strode towards him. The slow voice spoke again, near at hand.

'I am your son.'

Wærmund reached out into the darkness. His hands touched a big, firm-fleshed trunk, broad shoulders, muscular arms. His finger-tips drew a face he had seen a little while before he went blind. He clutched Offa's arms and rested his head for a moment on Offa's shoulder. Offa felt him shudder and gasp once; he put his arms round his father. Neither wept.

The king straightened and stepped back from his son's embrace. His face was stern.

'Why? Why have you kept this terrible silence, Offa? How could you do it?'

The household had been asking themselves the same question. They listened intently.

'When I was a child, I watched two English fight a Myrging. He'd come into Angeln by chance, following a boar he was hunting. He offered to take on the two of them together but they chose single combat. Then, when he'd got one of them down, the other stabbed him in the back.'

Offa stopped. The household waited, puzzled, for him to go on. He seemed to believe he had said all that was needed to explain himself.

In his blindness, Wærmund's other senses had sharpened. He could hear in the tones of a voice what the speaker was not saying in words. He had even learned to hear what was said in the silences between words. He listened now to Offa's silence.

The Myrgings had not raided Freawine's land during Offa's childhood. If they had, the prince would never have been taken from the women's bower to watch the fighting. But King Eadgils had ridden out hunting and had never been seen again.

Wærmund had no trouble guessing the names of Offa's two childhood companions who had killed Eadgils against all the laws of honour. He saw the terrible choice that Offa had to make while he was too young for such a burden. If he spoke of other things and never mentioned the killing, he would have made himself a partner in it. If he spoke about the killing, he would betray his foster-brothers and shame Freawine. So he had decided not to speak at all.

That was not the worst. A brave and generous man, a king, lay in an unmarked grave, without honour in dying and without his rites. Offa could not right that wrong, so he had buried himself in a living grave, without respect or friendship.

And now, after paying his childhood as wergild for Eadgils, he had pledged himself to go alone against two champions, to wipe out the disgrace on his folk.

There was nothing Wærmund could do to ransom Offa's lost youth. He must do his best to safeguard the rest of his son's life, short though it must be. He had one week.

'We'd better start your weapon-training,' was all he said.

They hunted through their precious store of mail-shirts for one to fit Offa. Most were clearly too small. He burst the links of the two they forced on him, just by trying to breathe. Only his father matched him in size. Wærmund ordered his own mail to be brought out. That masterpiece of smith's work was unwrapped from the oiled cloths in which it had lain for years. They got his arms in without straining. Offa said patiently that the byrnie would serve him very well. Wærmund passed his hands over his son's body and found that he was slightly hunching his shoulders and hollowing his chest.

'Cut it open down the left side and fasten it with straps. He'll have to cover the gap with his shield.'

The best swordsman in the war-band began to teach Offa the simplest lessons of sword-play, not to swing wildly, wasting his strength, missing his blows and leaving himself wide open to his enemy. The swordsman was used to callow boys threshing about; he got a surprise.

Offa had spent years watching Freawine's young warriors at their weapon-training, storing up every word and move. He knew how to hold a sword and where to aim his strokes. But he was desperately slow.

The swordsman struggled to find words to let Wærmund see something he himself had never seen before.

'Watching him is like listening to a scop reciting a lay about some old hero-fight. Offa's strong enough to kill a man with one blow and he knows just how to do it. But it's all thought-out, like a scop choosing the best words and linking them together. He takes too much time over it.'

Offa had too little time.

'Well, if he knows what to do with a sword, set two or three men on to him at once,' said Wærmund grimly. 'Don't give him time to think.'

There was another deadly flaw in Offa's swordsmanship, as well as his habit of stopping to think out every move. He could kill a man with one blow; he could also destroy a sword at one blow, he struck with such force. If he did not kill his man at once, he would likely leave himself weaponless.

'There was a sword worthy of him,' said Wærmund '– if I can still find it – if the rust hasn't eaten it already in its grave'.

He told them, as best he could, the way he had gone out on to the moors with Stedefæst. They found the barrow at last; his fingers groped for the runes on the stone. They counted the paces till they came to the right tree; his fingers scrabbled among its roots. They dug where he told them and Stedefæst was lifted into the light. The blade was already rusted; the swordsmith promised to do his best with it.

Wærmund forbade Offa to practise with it. 'If Stedefæst is broken before the deathblow, there's not another sword on Middle Earth that can help you.'

Messengers from Angeln had already gone to King Witta, to fix the meeting-place, on an island in the Eider between the English and Myrging lands. At that place the current rushed so fiercely through the Monster-Gate that there was neither bridge nor ford. The island could only be reached by boat, so there would be no danger that either side could get sudden help from friends on the river-bank.

The English envoys pledged themselves, in the name of King Wærmund and the Angelcynn, to keep the terms. If their man lost, they would yield their borderlands up to ten miles north of the Eider and pay wergild to the Myrgings. If he won, they would keep their lands and take as much wergild from the Myrgings as the Myrgings had claimed from them. They would also take hostages for peace-keeping. The fight would take place under the eyes and judgement of the Swabian king.

Witta was a shrewd man. He noted that the English had slightly shifted the moot-point from his claim of overlordship to a quarrel between English and Myrgings, with himself as the wise fair-minded judge. He liked the part. He felt he was heir to the dignity of the Roman Kaisers in the old times. He let the terms pass. Whatever the English said would make no difference. Everyone knew how the fight must end.

When Wærmund and Offa came down to the ferry-boat, both banks of the Eider were crowded where they overlooked the island. King Witta's high seat had been brought on a wagon; he sat there enthroned, looking over the heads of his warband. The Myrgings had come in throngs to cheer for the death of the English prince and the humbling of Angeln. On the English side, a good many nobles and warriors had come, heavy-hearted, out of loyalty to Wærmund. The farming folk were keeping well away, guessing that the Myrgings would be across the river once Offa fell.

Some strangers had arrived – Wærnas, Jutes, Frisians – drawn by curiosity, pity, or the sheer huntsman's joy of seeing a creature bayed and done to death. There were wild stories about Offa going from mouth to mouth, to give spice to the entertainment. Was he really a lack-wit? A mute? Was that huge young warrior really the old king's son – or Thunor in his shape, come to help the English? Even the members of Wærmund's own household, who had seen him and spoken with him, did not know what to make of Offa or what to expect of him.

Wærmund reached for his son's sword-hand, to touch it in farewell. He found it was holding a drawn sword; he cried out in alarm.

'That's not Stedefæst! What have you done with him?'

'He's in my scabbard, behind my shield.'

Offa sounded more cheerful than Wærmund had ever heard him.

'I mean to fight fair. There's no reason why I shouldn't be fair to myself as well as to the Myrgings. I can only use one sword and hit one of them at a time. Even if I've got a weapon for each of them, I'll still be holding our border single-handed.'

He stepped into the ferry-boat. Wærmund's boy led the king to his own chosen place. A stream came down into the Eider, just north of the island. It was wide and swift enough to need a foot-bridge. When they stood on the bridge, the boy would have a clear view of the fight and could describe it to his lord, undisturbed by shouts and scuffling.

Wærmund had another reason for placing himself on the bridge and telling the rest of his household to stand aloof on the bank, but he had not spoken about that.

The ferry-boat's prow grounded on the island. Offa stepped ashore; the ferryman pushed off, leaving him alone against his enemies. The two were already waiting for him. They did not budge, leaving him to walk forward and put himself within reach of their swords.

Meaca had come with his brother; he was looking forward to killing Wærmund's son with no risk to himself. When the English heard who the second swordsman was, they spat. Even some of the Myrgings, who had come to yell for his victory, muttered that no one could make a better second at a child-killing than Meaca. He had already slaughtered his kinsman Eadgils' sons.

The Myrgings struck at once. Offa parried their blades with his shield. He made no attempt to strike back. The brothers grinned at each other. So the rumours were true; old Wærmund's last get couldn't handle a sword. They set out to wear him down and bewilder him under a hail of blows. Fairly soon, one of them would get behind him, or his left arm would droop from the strain of their battering. Then they could run him through.

Wærmund had no need to listen to his boy. The sound of swords meeting a shield, never sword on sword; the roar of cheering from the south bank, the glum silence on the English side told him what was happening. He began to edge towards the far end of the bridge, where an eddy from the current swirling downstream had scooped out a deep pool. When Offa fell, so would he.

But it was taking the Myrgings a long time to tire Offa and break his guard. As a child he had run beside Freawine's horse, or raced ahead with the hounds in full cry, because no one had dared to let him ride. He stood in the ring when the quarry was brought to bay, alert to dodge at the last moment of safety, when the boar charged or the stag swung its antlers. Now, his big lungs were still breathing easily. In spite of his size and weight, he was quick enough to block the Myrgings' every move.

So they began to goad him, to draw his attention from their swords to their words, to make him so angry that he rushed at them and started to flail with his sword-arm.

They called him a mooncalf, an old man's sapless get, without the wit to wipe his nose or his backside, let alone use a sword. They told him his mother had made up for her husband's withered tail-tree by whoring with etins in the forest to get herself with child. That was why Offa was such a monstrous sackful of offal, he'd split her to the navel being born.

Offa had spent his childhood listening to Freawine's men talking about him. That had been worse, because they had not meant to hurt him or even knew he heard. They simply thought he was born a lack-wit and that being lack-witted meant being deaf as well as dumb. There was nothing the Myrgings could say now that could get through his guard.

The brothers had slackened their attacks to have breath for their insults. Offa used the respite planning how to separate the pair and deciding which he would take first. He chose Mearcweard, as the more dangerous, likely to give most trouble. Destroying Mearcweard might cost two swords; he would rather tackle Meaca, if he had to do it with only his shield and his bodily strength.

Having made up his mind, he joined in the talk.

'When I told you to bring a friend, Mearcweard, I didn't know you hadn't got any – that you'd have to beg your elder brother to stand up for you, just when he thought he'd found a use for you. He was glad enough to pack you off to the Swabians as a hostage. But you're not giving your new master much return either today, for the food and straw he allows you.'

Offa took in everything he saw. He had noted how much Mearcweard hated the word '*master*' and guessed that he resented being held as a hostage, was bitter that his brother had handed him over, even though he had no choice.

The words were spoken flatly, without much interest. Offa's tone said clearly that Mearcweard was not worth the trouble of losing one's temper. He stood looking at Mearcweard, bored, his unused sword dangling from his fingers.

Mearcweard could not stand him. He charged. Offa seemed taken aback, unable to move. Mearcweard swung his sword up, ready to hack through Offa's right shoulder and take off his sword-arm. For a moment, his own right side was unguarded.

In that moment, Offa stepped neatly to the left to avoid him, but struck out at the same time with a back-handed slash as Mearcweard, unable to check or change direction, hurtled past. Offa had placed his blow; the blade went in under the rib-cage, slicing through mail, flesh and guts. When it met the spine it was shattered but so was Mearcweard's back. He crashed to the ground.

Wærmund heard his boy cry out. The cry – almost a shriek – echoed all around him from the English bank. He stepped towards the edge of the bridge.

The boy yelled, 'Mearcweard's down! He's killed Mearcweard!' then, terrified, 'Take care, my lord – *step back!*'

Wærmund tottered – then felt hands clutching him. He was shaking but he let himself be guided. A small hand gripped his and kept hold of it. He knew he would have to take the boy with him if he drowned himself.

On the island, Meaca stared at his brother's body, struggling with his shock, his grief for the one man he had trusted – and with his fear. He had never tackled an enemy before without armed companions to back him.

He looked uneasily at Offa, who was watching him with no sign of triumph.

'There's your younger brother, down in the dirt where you belong. You got out of the womb in front of him, but you've skulked behind him ever since.'

Offa was holding Meaca's eyes, so that he was no longer looking down at his brother's body. He shifted his position very slightly back towards his right. Meaca, frozen by his cold voice, did not notice.

'You'd always rather let others do your killing for you, so they say. Yes, I know you slew King Eadgils' sons, but that was at a friendly meeting. They didn't have their swords.'

'And neither have you!'

Meaca pointed his own weapon at the fragment of blade, broken off near the hilt that Offa was still holding. He laughed as he darted in to the kill. Offa dropped his useless weapon. Meaca lunged forward. Offa chose his moment to draw Stedefæst; the gold and garnets on the hilt flamed across Meaca's eyes in the noon-day sun.

Meaca stumbled. He had killed his kin, it was just that his kin should help Offa to kill him. He tripped over Mearcweard's feet and spitted himself on Stedefæst.

King Witta, glad to show himself unconcerned in the Myrgings' defeat, played his part as fair-minded judge of the combat and forbade any more fighting. He sent some of his men to fetch the corpses and hand them over to their own people. The Myrgings would not be needing another chief; he would take care of their land. He would deal with the English another time.

When Wærmund's men came for Offa, they found him by the southern shore of the island, drawing Stedefæst's blade through the Eider. He lifted the glittering sword, clean of Meaca's blood, to greet them.

'I've just drawn our border. The boundary-line stays here.'

The English Language:
Continuity and Change

Stephen Pollington

History is characterised by a sense of narrative, of a chain of events, the rise and fall of societies and the growth and decay of trends. History is in every sense a *story*, an unfolding tale in which characters and events are set against their respective backgrounds. Herein lies the essential disappointment of archaeology and its associated disciplines: for all the potsherds, pins and pennies that the diggers turn up, they are seldom if ever able to say anything at all about the story behind them. To take a famous example, the Coppergate Helmet has been studied from almost every scientific angle imaginable, but no-one has been able to answer the obvious questions: Why was it hidden in a carefully sealed layer of soil in York? Who owned it, who made it, who wore it, who hid it? These are questions which it is perhaps unfair of us to expect archaeologists to answer, yet they frame the essential, human character of the find. We are all more interested in human actions and motives than in the sterile assessment of means.

We are fortunate in this country to have the names recorded of many hundreds of persons from more than a thousand years ago, who settled and owned estates here. The search for these individuals is in every sense the search for the roots of England, though it is as often conducted in libraries as in the fields. English place-names carry the story of the country within them, whether they are old names or new ones. The relatively modern idea of naming a street after a local councillor, political leader or dignitary echoes the Victorian equivalent, whereby almost every English town has a 'Nelson Road', 'Trafalgar Avenue' and so on. Even modern mock-Tudor housing developments are commonly given names such as 'Badgers Croft' or 'The Maltings', perpetuating the name of the feature which was destroyed to make way for them. Landscape names such us Gallows Hill, Chalk Pit Farm, Oak Ridge, Rushmere, Broomfield, Eastwood need only a second's thought to determine their meaning. Such names may have been given at any time up to the present day, although they may sometimes be surprisingly ancient. Harder to interpret are names such as Appledore, unless you happen to know that *apulder* is an old word for 'apple tree'. Such a name must go back to the time when *apulder* was a common word for 'apple tree', since otherwise it would have conveyed no meaning to the people who gave and used the name. Here we begin to address the nature of historical records.

If we start to trace our local or national history through its written documentation, as well as through the gathering of information from the landscape and the buildings and settlements within it, we very soon confront the fact of linguistic change. As dated as the works of Charles Dickens or Sir Walter Scott may feel to us now, they are easier for us to read than those of Samuel Johnson, or Jonathan Swift, or William

Shakespeare. This is because the greater the distance in time the writer and his text are from us, the more different is his usage, the less familiar his words and the uses to which he puts them.

So with local records, where difficulties in language and script multiply the further back we trace our story. For the 15th century, the language in our written texts is barely recognisable as English; a century earlier, the differences in some records are so great that we think in terms of a different language 'Middle English', with a substantially different grammar. By the eleventh century, further changes mean we must speak of Old English, with more-or-less copious records extending back to the eighth century. Beyond that, the records are few and difficult to interpret, the language of early Old English is more ancient in character, the physical documents rarer (more often existing as appendices copied into later documents) and less confident in its prosody. By the seventh century, with a few exceptions surviving as place names in Latin ownership documents, records of English are mostly not written in Roman letters at all, but occur in runes, the native script, graven into wood or metal or stone.

If we press on beyond the sixth century, the complete absence of written records is striking, and by the fourth there is a fundamental change: texts in any form of English are non-existent here, the language of the occasional monumental inscriptions is Latin (often with specific insular characteristics) and the *milieu* of writing is 'official' – ecclesiastical, governmental and commercial. A watershed is passed in the fifth century, a point of transition. This should not be surprising: 4th century Britain was a more-or-less autonomous province within a large empire. By the mid 5th c. the old order had changed, there were new political forces in the land, and the foundations of what was to become England were already in place before the century ended.

From the 5th to the 21st century is linguistically a comparatively straight line, with occasional blips along the way to accommodate increased exposure to Norse (9th to 10th c.), Norman French (11th to 12th c.) and the revived classical languages of Greece and Rome (16th c.). However, despite all the obvious signs of imported words in our language, the core is remarkably consistent in time. It is still not possible to construct any length of meaningful English without using words familiar to the first settlers of the 5th c. King Alfred, writing in the late ninth century, says:

Gemunde ic eac hu ic geseah ... ða ciricean giond eall Angelcynn stodon

Allowing for spelling and the changes of more than a thousand years, most of these same words would be used today:

I minded also how I saw ... the churches stood throughout all England

(The old word *eke* from Old English *eac* 'also' has all but disappeared, and *yond* no longer means 'across' although *be-yond* still means 'on the other side'.) Interestingly, Alfred does not actually refer to the 'English land' but, rather, to the 'English kin' or 'nation', showing clearly that in his day the English were felt to be a distinct group of people by birth – 'kin' or family. The choice of ethnonym *Angel* 'Angle, Anglian' is the more surprising since Alfred and his people were not Anglian by extraction, but Saxon; he was *Wesseaxna cyning* 'king of the West Saxons'.

Often these core words from Old English are more emotive, more expressive, more meaningful than the florid and learned terms borrowed from elsewhere. The use of Latin- and Greek-based terminology became a sign of good education, and eventually acquired a snob value quite out of proportion to its only real purpose, the use of such terms in science where their absence of secondary and related meanings makes them useful in referring to one thing only. We may feel that a 'cordial reception' (French from Latin) is pleasant enough, if a little formal and sterile, but it is no substitute for a 'hearty welcome' (straight from Old English).

Few foreign words have actually succeeded in penetrating to the heart of the language, and those which have are most often the short, punchy words which harmonise well with English patterns of speech. 'Ear', 'eye', 'nose', 'mouth', 'brow', 'lip', 'nostril', 'cheek', 'tongue', 'tooth', 'hair' and 'beard' are all of Old English origin, but 'face' is taken from French – possibly because it fitted better than the two native words: *neb* which could also mean 'nose', and *andwlita* which was a little long and cumbersome.

Armed with a rudimentary knowledge of the language, a good dictionary and reliable copies of local records, it is possible for the interested reader to establish a pattern of local place-names from the Old English period. (This is not always possible for every district, especially in areas where there has been heavy outside settlement, e.g. Welsh, Norman French, and especially Norse.) Of course, not all names would necessarily have been in use throughout the period: for example, A name such as Edwalton (Nottinghamshire) from Old English *eadwaldes tun* 'Eadwald's estate' records just one owner of land that was probably under cultivation and in the ownership of English-speakers for centuries. We cannot tell for sure whether Eadwald held the land in the eleventh century or the seventh. If the name of the estate changed every time the owner changed, this argues for Eadwald as the last pre-Conquest owner; however, such a procedure would have been quite confusing, and possibly the name changed only if the boundaries were extended or altered in a significant way. Nevertheless, our farmer of a thousand or more years ago was once so strongly associated with this particular piece of land that the link to his name has remained in place through all the changes and upheavals of the intervening millennium.

Not all English place-names are what they seem: Lincoln, for example, is taken from the Roman name for the city: *Lindum Colonia*. This backs up place-name and archaeological evidence that there were Germanic settlements around the city during the last years of Roman administration, where the men were granted settlement rights on marginal land in exchange for their services in protecting the villas and trading posts of the wealthy native Romano-Britons. Names of this type are usually cited as evidence for continuity of Romano-British society, settlement and population into early Anglo-Saxon times. Yet, when the name is first written down by an English-speaker (Bede, c.730), it has the form *Lindocolina*. Written as one word, the name has ceased to have any meaning (it was originally British *lindon* 'pool', to which the Roman title *colonia* 'colony' was added); the classically trained Bede would surely have restored Latin *colonia* if he could have recognised it in this word. A century and a half later, someone thought they could understand the name – the *Anglo-Saxon Chronicle* (c.890) has *Lindcylene* which looks like a rationalisation to *lindcylene* linden – kiln, a kiln which burns limewood. Lincoln is not alone: York began as *eborakon* 'yew tree place', was adopted into Latin as *Eboracum*, then anglicised to *Eoforwic* 'boar farm' before being seized by Scandinavians and transformed to *Iorvik*, and so *Iorek* and York.

The study of history demonstrates that the story of this island is characterised by the interplay of opposing forces: stasis and dynamism, or the tendency for things to remain as they are and the opposing tendency for things to evolve through time. The story of Britain as a whole shows long static periods (one does not say 'stagnation') during which things seem to have proceeded for decades, even centuries, with little in the way of change in people's lives, punctuated by bursts of immense change, even turmoil, in which things must often have seemed completely unstable, as the certainties of one generation were overturned by its successor. However much historians may argue for Englishness as an invented or adopted identity; for population replacement or continuity; for rural depopulation or the survival of Romano-British villa estates; one fact is undisputed and one thread is constant through the centuries: the English language came to dominate quickly and comprehensively across large areas of lowland Britain between the 4th and 6th centuries, and that language, surprisingly little changed, has remained dominant through all the subsequent invasions, social upheavals, turmoil and commotion.

This fact of linguistic continuity is difficult to explain under some present models of the English settlement. If relatively few people actually crossed the sea and settled in these islands, how is it that their language came to dominate, and to root itself so firmly in the land that centuries of foreign domination and deliberate suppression could not eradicate it? We know that the Germanic-speaking Franks entered a land where Latin and Celtic were spoken, just as the English did. They dominated the social structure, but within a few generations their speech was a derivative of Latin, Old French, and only their personal names and a few vocabulary items show their original Germanic affiliation. Our story in Britain should be similar elite domination followed by progressive loss of identity, culminating in total absorption. This did not happen. The usual objection is the hypothesis that native Romano-Britons were swamped with Anglo-Saxon culture and had to re-invent themselves in a new Germanic guise if they were to survive. This is an interesting assumption, since if the numbers of English migrants were small, it is hard to see how they could force or persuade whole regional populations to switch cultural identities. In fact, not only do we find the English language and way of life replacing their late Romano-British equivalents, the presence of occasional British names among the English (e.g. West Saxon kings Cerdic, Ceawlin, Cadwalla) suggests that when Britons did merge with Anglo-Saxons, they retained their own personal names and thus their cultural identities.

There are good reasons to study the processes of language change I have outlined above, to grasp the directions of change and to understand the processes. Not the least important reason is that they give access to the original literature which is often crucial in understanding history and culture. Knowledge of Old and Middle English opens up vast areas of study and interpretation, which can only enrich understanding of both the past and the present. This knowledge re-connects us to the story-so-far, and throws new light on the language we use today. It is the one secure thread that links so many millions around the world to this land and its people, more immediately than any political or social constructs, any commercial or religious entities, the language we use is the very raw material of our thought. That, surely, is worthy of our greatest efforts towards understanding.

The Resurrection of England

Fr. Andrew Phillips

Ever the faith endures, England, my England.

W. E. Henley

Foreword: Not British, but English

A nation which has forgotten its past can have no future.

Sir Winston Churchill

And yet again the tabloids scream out their headlines: 'British football thugs terrorise tourists'. 'French police attack football animals'. 'Youth stabbed in stadium shock'. Yes, another report about foreign café-owners and shopkeepers, their premises vandalised and ravaged, moaning about British yobs, about 'the British disease'. Although I am ashamed of such behaviour, I feel no personal shame, for I am one of those who is *not British, but English*. Let me explain.

For me as an Englishman, football hooligans are simply following in the footsteps of a long line of *British* thugs, some of whom, incredibly enough, have even been glorified by *British* historians. In the end is there really much difference between the murderous yobs who ended thirty-nine lives at the Heysel stadium in Belgium in 1985 and Rhodes in Africa and Clive in India? What difference between racist thugs in London and the international hooliganism of imperialist exploitation? And before Rhodes and Clive, there was many a pirate and buccaneer, the tattooed and ear-ringed skinheads and racists of their age, who terrorised the Caribbean with their thuggery. And before them...

But this is only an introduction. Before I get into detail, let me simply sum up what has been said so far: I am not, either by background, or by choice, British. I am the member of an oppressed minority, the English, a minority that has for centuries been spiritually oppressed by the very concept of 'the British'. And as to how this dichotomy of British and English arose, then I invite you to read on.

The Tragedy of English History

a) The Confusion

And who held the power of England. The elderly, pear-headed, self-willed German, often mad and always stupid, who wondered how the apple got inside the dumpling. And working with him were the few, corrupt and evil families engaged in the enslavement of the English poor.

John Masefield, *The War and the Future*

Although the eighteenth century did not invent the British myth, it certainly did much to develop its jingoistic potential. The eighteenth century was after all much busied with building an Empire. And which had been the greatest Empire to date? Why, of course, that of the Romans: hence the use of the Latin name of this country in 'Rule Britannia' (and not Rule England) and the invocation, always used by blackguards to justify their base aims, of the Deity: 'God save the King' – regardless of, or perhaps because of, the fact that he was a depraved fool. This was after all the age in which Dr. Johnson noted that patriotism had become the last refuge of the scoundrel.

This eighteenth century Empire began with the Hanoverians sending their Gestapo-like troops into the Scottish Highlands 'to clear them', or, as we would say nowadays, to ethnically cleanse them. But really it was even worse than that, for those cleared were not replaced by human beings, but with sheep. Such was the value placed on human life by the German kings of England and 'the few, corrupt and evil families' who supported them. God save them indeed. This was not 'Enlightenment', rather the 'Dark Ages'. But then are we really to say that all had been sweetness and light in the preceding century?

The seventeenth century. That age of civil war and the age of that genocidal tyrant, Cromwell, that British Lenin. It is his statue, an unbearable provocation to all free men and women everywhere, that stands arrogantly, but also typically, outside the *British* Houses of Parliament. But that dictator and mass murderer was followed by that lewd pseudo-Frenchman Charles II and then the tyrannical James II and then that stupid Dutchman William who had no business here anyway.

So, I hear you say, if you do not like the Germans of the eighteenth or the Dutchman, or the Scottish Stuarts of the seventeenth, then you are a lover of the Welsh Tudors.

No, I do not love the Tudors, blood-soaked murderers and murderesses, burners of martyrs, typified by greed and lust incarnate, Henry VIII, Henry the Syphilitic.

Ah, I hear you say, he loves the Middle Ages, he is a Francophile, a mediaevalist.

b) The Curse

> There was a year, I understand,
> A thousand odd since Christ the King,
> There reigned three kings in England
> Ere Christmas bells were due to ring;
> And after them came never a one
> Of English blood of song to sing.
>
> Maurice Hewlett, *The Song of the Plow*

Oh no. All those Frenchmen who ruled us in the Middle Ages were tainted with the curse of the Norman Bastard, William, born of the Harlot, responsible for the greatest genocide in European history until the Crusades.

What can we say of William the Viking usurper who, having laid waste the south of England, proceeded to the north and, according to *Orderic Vitalis*, killed a hundred thousand? Hovedon wrote: 'It was a horrible spectacle to see on the high roads and public places, and at the doors of houses, human bodies eaten by the worms, for there remained no-one to cover them with a little earth'. What can we say of William the barbarian invader who, as the Anglo-Saxon Chronicle put it, 'built castles far and wide throughout the land, filled with devils and wicked men, oppressing the unhappy people'? This man and all his progeny were cursed.

There was the Conqueror's son, Rufus the depraved. There was his brother Henry, who invented drawing and quartering, who put out the eyes of his other brother Robert by pouring a basinful of red-hot metal into them, who had the eyes of two grand-daughters put out and their noses cut off. Then there was his cruel and faithless daughter, Matilda, who with her feeble French cousin Stephen reduced England to nineteen long winters of civil war. It was then that the Anglo-Saxon Chronicle recorded: 'Men said openly that Christ and His Saints slept. Evil reigned in the land'.

Shall we go on to recount the occupation of Ireland by Matilda's son, Henri d'Anjou (or Henry II as he is called), who had the Archbishop of Canterbury slain at the altar? Shall we speak of all those Anglo-Norman castle-builders, who having oppressed and subjugated England, oppressed Wales, Scotland, Ireland and then much of France in 'The Hundred Years War'? And not content with that, they also set off to the Holy Land and by bankrupting the English peasantry, slaughtered Muslim, Jew and Christian alike, until Jerusalem and Constantinople were awash with blood.

No wonder all these Norman 'nobles', 'the few, corrupt and evil families', whose descendants long sat in, or rather *occupied* the House of Lords, took as their heraldic emblems the tokens of their savagery: dogs' heads, bulls' heads, boars' heads, daggers, swords, clubs, fiery dragons, crazed griffons, drunken bears, mad rams, cunning foxes, evil hyenas, ruthless wolves, everything that was hellish and bestial, bloodthirsty and raging.

So much for the 'superior civilisation' of the Normans who saddled England and all the other peoples of these poor islands with their 'Establishment'. It was their bureaucratic centralisation that began with their Tower of London and Whitehall. Under the Normans the historic capital of England went from Winchester to London, the Great Wen of the future, York was pillaged and Canterbury spiritually gutted.

The Norman imperialists after all were the real inventors of the 'British' imperialist myth. A myth in their own bloodied image. For why else did they devise the myth of Arthur, the 'romance' that fictionalised the Romano-Celtic war-leader? This their myth

39

was a mere device to deprive the English of our own real heroes, like Alfred, who had regained England for the English from the cousins of the Normans, the Danes. It was a myth devised to deprive the English of their own spiritual culture, their own nobility, their own civilisation. It was the beginning of that Establishment myth which has so oppressed the English to this day, to such an extent that many of the so-called English actually identify themselves with 'the British'. Sad to say most of my compatriots are not English patriots, they have been bought out by the Establishment. And although there are those of us who continue to work for the English Resistance, Francis Brett Young was right when he wrote in 'The Island':

> Cold heart and bloody hand
> Now rule fair England.

Now I can hear some readers saying, 'Ah, I understand, this writer is a racist: everything that is Norman is bad, everything that is English is good'. Not so, say I. For if I were a racist, I could not be anti-Norman. The Normans by race were as Germanic as the English. True, the pagan warbands assembled under the Normans were composed not only of Norman thieves, but of all the dross of Western Europe, from Brittany and Flanders, from all parts of France and even from Germany and Italy, and their common language was the lowest of Latin. But they were Norman-led.

Neither is the author among those who believe that before 1066 all was well in England, and that after all was ill. There is little black and white in history, far more light grey and dark grey. And England had been betrayed by at least some of its leaders before 1066. In any case for many of us the legitimate royal house had already ended in 1016 with the tragic and suspicious death of the English hero Edmund Ironside.

And then I am no lover of those primitive Germanic tribesmen who came to these shores in the fifth century, and chased out or enslaved or intermarried with and absorbed the Romano-Britons.

Writer, you have demolished myths, you have deconstructed – what is left? Who are the English if they are not a race? What is the identity, the soul of this land? What is the Spirit of England? What then is Englishness?

Englishness

a) The English Soul

> True hearts are more than coronets,
> And simple faith than Norman blood.

> Alfred Lord Tennyson

Any national identity, such as Englishness, is created firstly by factors which are more or less fixed. These are climate and geography.

It is clear that the temperate and moderate climate of England have influenced the general English character. This does not resemble the character of those further north, often made morose by the harshness of their climate and the darkness of their latitudes. Equally, our character does not resemble the exuberance of those who live further south where the sun burns hot.

Secondly, we live in a country that is largely flat, where the sea is never very far away. We do not have that arduous character so common among mountain-peoples. Neither do we have that character common to peoples who live on large, continental expanses of land, where summers are boiling and winters freezing. No, we are island-dwellers. This fact accounts for some major part of our distinctive character – our insularity. Those who live on islands are by definition insular and cannot be otherwise. And one of those insular characteristics is reserve. It matters not what island you visit, Sicily, Cyprus, Malta, Corsica or even Japan, islanders are people of reserve. For if you openly disagree on an island, you will not be able to go somewhere else, you will have to moderate your views, compromise or else conceal your disagreement. Hence the phlegm of the English and the inscrutability of the Japanese.

But now I hear my reader saying: 'Then in that case why are all people who live on islands with similar climates not similar? Why are the English and the Japanese not identical? Why are the Corsican and the Cypriot not the same?' Because there is a third and decisive element that must be taken into account when describing that general assembly of characteristics that we loosely call 'national identity', that set of beliefs that determines any given way of life. This element is essential to the identity and character of any people, for it determines their social, political and cultural life. It is the underlying Faith or set of spiritual beliefs of a people which determines how it lives to an even greater extent than climate or geography. Only this can explain why, for example, the Japanese and the English or, even more strikingly, the Cypriots and the Corsicans, differ.

How else are we to explain the gulf that separates such a figure as Cromwell, the archetypal Puritan dictator, and, on the other hand, a figure such as Thomas à Becket? The first, the seventeenth-century dictator, unlikeable and unliked, tyrannised and murdered those who did not accept him. Eventually he died alone and miserable – as he had lived. The second, though hardly a man of honest or chaste background, was Archbishop of Canterbury in an England that enjoyed life, that had music and fun, that feasted and was alive. And yet both were Englishmen. The difference, of course, is that the latter was a strong and fanatical Roman Catholic and the former a strong and fanatical Protestant.

Not, personally, that I have a preference for either. Cromwell was a tyrant and a killjoy who banned Christmas and desecrated churches. Becket was the venal representative of an organisation become a medieval con-trick, that had first arranged for the subjugation of England by its Norman shock-troops and then bled it for taxes.

Becket's death was little more than a medieval gangland killing, as rival groups jostled for power and privilege. And when England, under the diabolical French glutton King John, no longer paid taxes or homage to the tyrant in Rome, the same tricksters thereupon excommunicated the land and its people. (The Roman Catholic Church was merely the medieval equivalent of the modern EU; join us or face economic excommunication).

What I am saying is that England's basic values radically changed with the Reformation. Political beliefs changed, social beliefs changed, cultural beliefs changed, because spiritual and therefore moral beliefs changed. A whole culture changed. *British* Protestantism made way for individualism, the Industrial Revolution, colonial genocide and exploitation and all our modernity with its World Wars, nuclear and ecological Apocalypse Now 'culture'. Before and after the Reformation climate and geography did not change – and yet most of England and the English did change, because beliefs changed.

However, long before the sixteenth century Reformation, the Norman Invaders, as we have already seen, had already transformed England. The basic values of English culture, the Faith of the English, had already been transformed in the eleventh century *Deformation* of the Normans. They had already changed the Faith of our forebears, the Faith that had become the *English* Faith long before ever Norman had spoken in this land, and in ways far more radical than the sixteenth century Reformation. This means that if England and the English soul are to be understood, we have to take a far longer, more *radical* view. We have to get behind and beyond the Normans, to the *authentic roots* of English culture and beliefs in the first 500 years of our existence as a nation.

b) The English Faith

> Day breaks on England down the Kentish hills,
> Singing in the silence of the meadow-footing rills,
> Day of my dreams, O day!
> I saw them marching from Dover, long ago,
> With a silver cross before them, singing low.
>
> J. E. Flecker.

The Faith that became the English Faith came to the English from over the sea, from Jerusalem via Ireland, Gaul and Rome.

From a racist point of view, it was a foreign Faith: racially Christ in His human nature was a Jew, though that did not prevent his compatriots from having Him crucified. And those who brought the Faith to the English and some of those who deepened it were foreign. Foreign, nay, exotic, influences abounded. St Augustine, like St Laurence, St Justus, St Paulinus and St Honorius, was Italian. St Mellitus, the first Bishop of London whose life is recorded in any detail, was probably a Sicilian Greek. St Felix, the Apostle of East Anglia, was a Burgundian. St Birinus, Apostle of Wessex, was a

Lombard. St Aidan, the Apostle of the North, was Irish. St Cuthbert wore a pectoral cross with at its centre a shell from the Indian Ocean. St Agilbert of Dorchester was a Frank. St Theodore of Canterbury, he who created the beginnings of national consciousness, was a Greek. St Edfrith, illuminating the Lindisfarne Gospels, used ink made from lapus lazuli from the Himalayas. St Ives of Huntingdonshire was a Persian. St Oda of Canterbury, like St Oswald of York, was a Dane. But once the English had received the Faith, they made it their own.

Moreover, this English Faith, the Faith of our forebears, the Faith of Oswald, Cedd, Chad, Cuthbert, Audrey, Hilda, Mildred, Benedict, Wilfrid, Aldhelm, Guthlac, Bede, Willibrord, Boniface, Swithin, Edmund, Edgar, Edward, Edith, Dunstan and a host of others, was part of the Universal Christian Faith, of a Commonwealth and Confederation, of a Family that stretched from Asia and Africa through Europe to America, from Vinland to Finland, from Sweden to Sudan, from Ireland to India. This is the Faith which provided this land and this people with its Saints, giving a spiritual personality and identity, a soul, to England. This Faith is the only variable element in Englishness, and it happens to be the spiritual component of Englishness. England's soul is made of those who in Faith hallowed the land, who made it sacred, endowing it with unity and diversity, with spiritual and therefore moral reality. These Saints of England provided the English with enduring values, with a soul, with a Faith. This was the Faith of the so-called 'Anglo-Saxon', or rather, Old English, Church, which we shall now describe in detail.

The Secret of English History

O Faith of England, taught of old
By faithful shepherds of the fold,
The hallowing of our nation...
Our fathers heard the trumpet call
Through lowly cot and kingly hall
From overseas resounding.
Our fathers held the faith received,
By saints declared, by saints believed,
By saints in death defended.

T. A. Lacey

The Old English Church is virtually unknown today. It is the well-guarded secret of English history, which is nevertheless there for all those who seek it. What were and are its values?

a) Unity

Firstly, the Old English Church existed before the divisions of the eleventh century, when the Papacy cut itself off from the majority of Christians who then lived in the

Middle East and Eastern Europe. It existed before the further bloody divisions of the sixteenth century. It existed before the further subdivision of Western Europe into Roman Catholic South and Protestant North. In other words, in Old English times there was no 'ecumenism', because there were no denominations – the Church was basically One. Old English Christians were in full communion with the rest of Christendom, from Dublin to Damascus, from Winchester to Kiev, from Constantinople to Naples, from Rome to Jerusalem.

This Unity of Christendom existed basically because the Church in the West had not yet moved away from its roots, the Early Church. The Gospel Tradition, the lives of the Apostles and the Martyrs and the Fathers, the life of the Early, sincere Church, were all living realities. The Church in the West had not yet been overlaid with reasonings and speculations, distortions and institutions. In other words the Old English Church was pre-Scholastic, just as it was pre-Romanesque, because it was pre-Schism.

It did not know therefore of the excesses of the Middle Ages – indulgences, inquisitions, burnings at the stake, Crusades, legalism and hair-splitting. And so it did not know either of the excesses of those who were later to protest at medieval abuses, the puritanical Protestants of the 16th century with their iconoclasm and rejection of the Saints and the whole Church Tradition of the First Millennium. Because the Old English Church was both pre-Reformation and pre-Medieval, the mutual slaughter of 'Christians' by 'Christians', such as that of the sixteenth century, was simply unknown and unthinkable for it. The Old English Church has then a twofold attraction – it is One and Apostolic.

b) Life

Secondly, Old English Church life was not the abstract, dusty philosophy of the Medieval Schoolmen, it was a living and mystical reality in the daily lives of all. God was known not from speculative booklore, but from a direct, straightforward, immediate contact. The Saints had not been reduced to folklore and fable by forgers of fictional legends, they were real. People could say, 'I have met a Saint of God'.

The Old English period has over 300 Saints, who were close to the people because they were the people. They were the friends of the people who consoled them by helping and healing them. People knew what the Saints looked like from the frescoes covering the church walls – no cold, killjoy, white walls here. Relics had not been faked as they would be later, and the relics of the Saints helped people in their daily needs. The Virgin Mary had not been distorted into a distant goddess as in the Medieval Church, She was still the Mother of all, the Mother of the Church.

The church building and worship were mystical. Before the Gothic style ('Scholasticism in stone') with its spires pointing skywards to the lost God, people worshipped in candle-lit churches with small, round-headed windows, where God's presence was felt. They used a mystical, sacred language, with sacraments. Theology was not out of dry books, but out of living hearts, theology was life, contained in the services and prayerful experience.

Church teachings, explained in the vernacular (into which the Gospels had been translated) were not hurtful or categorical statements made by people in ivory towers. Teachings were spiritual revelations made to help people live. Theology and life, piety and experience, theory and practice, teachings and mysticism were all one. Old English Christianity, not in spite of being mystical, but because it was mystical, was a way of life, it patterned daily life. The rhythms of daily life were based on a liturgical pattern of fast and feast. Fasting, what today we call 'dieting' or 'healthy eating', came naturally. But I emphasise fast and feast. Christianity was joyful, there was none of that killjoy 'pious' and 'religious' attitude of mournful, 'constipated' Christianity that we owe to the deformations of the Middle Ages and Puritanism, especially the Victorian sort. There was fast and feast, the sorrow of the Crucifixion was followed directly by the joy of the Resurrection. There was no 'pie in the sky' of the Protestant moralisers. Heaven began on Earth for all those who wanted to live according to the rhythms of Church life – and for most of the Old English period, most Old English did.

c) Community

Thirdly, although of course there was a hierarchy in the Church, just as there was in secular life, just as there is in every human society, there was no clericalism. The average parish priest was a villager who was married, he was a family man, often his sons would become priests in their turn and his daughters priests' wives. And no doubt most people were very happy with this arrangement – 'the priest is one of us.' A married priesthood had a most natural attitude to women. The Old English Church was pre-Puritan. Some historians have suggested that the Old English Church allowed divorce and remarriage under the influence of St Theodore of Canterbury.

It can be said then that the Old English Church was part of a Family of Churches, uniting clergy and people, the living and the departed. Thus everybody belonged to the Church, a Church that was homely, because it was part of everyday life, of family life. Rich and poor belonged, King and peasant. Even physically, people stood united in church (pews and seats were the innovation of a much later period). There was no real division between priest and people, the priest and the other clergy. The deacons who played an important role were of the people and the people belonged to the royal priesthood.

The whole family belonged to the Church. Shortly after birth, babies were baptised and as soon as possible confirmed and given communion. (Confirmation in childhood was unthinkable, it would be the result of later medieval rationalism). Everybody received communion in both kinds – the reservation of the Blood of Christ for the clergy against the words of Christ Himself, was a later result of clericalism. Since the parish clergy were married, there was no condescension towards women – another result of clericalism and then of Puritanism with its dualistic contempt for the body and material world. (The important role of women in Old English life has been made clear in many learned studies, starting with that of Doris Stenton's, *The English Woman in History*, 1956). The Communion Service or 'Maesse' (a lovely word we have still kept in Christmas, Michaelmas, Martinmas, Candlemas, Childermas and the rarer Johnmas, Crouchmas and All-Hallowmas) was something that all could participate in. But the Church was not only homely, it was also otherworldly. This may sound paradoxical, but the combination of these two aspects is simply due to the Old English belief that the Son of God had become man, that Heaven had come down to Earth, the spiritual world had met the material one. And this was so that the material world could rise up to the spiritual one, the earthly to the heavenly, that men could become divine; homely, family – but also mystical, otherworldly. For the Old English Church was a family which united the living and the departed, bringing rich spiritual comfort and warmth to both.

d) Common Wealth

Finally, the Churches of Western Europe in Old English times resembled more a family than a pyramid. Clergy and people of God were united in this Common Wealth of Faith. Since the Old English Church was pre-Medieval, it was also pre- 'Papist'. I do not mean to say that the Old English Church had no respect for Rome and the Papacy. On the contrary, the Old English had enormous veneration for St Peter – judging by Church dedications, the most popular Saint. Moreover they had great respect for Rome. It was largely thanks to the saintly Pope Gregory the Great that the Old English had become Christians. Our forebears respected the Popes because they were representatives or 'vicars' of St Peter. (The term 'Vicar of Christ' was an invention of Hildebrand, Pope Gregory VII, 1073–1085, the fanatic who enforced clerical celibacy, the real founder of the Medieval Papacy and practice of Papal primacy and hegemony, of 'Papism'). Rome was respected because it was a City of Saints, a treasure house of holy relics, not because it was a centre of legal, political, economic or military power. The Old English flocked to Rome, that City of Martyrs, on pilgrimage. The Old English respected the Papacy precisely because it was not Papism.

The Popes did not generally interfere in the lives of the local Metropolitan Churches of Western Europe which were in their jurisdiction. True, the Archbishops of Canterbury had to go to Rome to receive the mark of their office, the pallium, but this was little more than a symbolic ritual. And if Popes did try and interfere, they generally did not get their way, as was the case during the episcopates of St Theodore and St Dunstan of Canterbury. The Popes were respected not because they were Popes (of whom some might be Saints, but others decidedly not), but because they sat on the Apostolic throne of St Peter.

The Churches of Western Europe at this time resembled more sovereign States joined together in a Confederation or Family of Faith. No violence was done to local Churches by distant, meddling absolutists in Rome or elsewhere. Interference and intervention would only begin with the new, reformed Papacy, which in 1054 separated itself from the Church, and then in 1066 under Alexander II, blessed the Norman Invasion of England. Thus it manipulated Norman lust for power, greed and stupidity in the hope of later being able to interfere in English life – which was indeed the case. Indeed the Papally-sponsored Normans and their descendants did not later hesitate to carry their oppression from England into Wales and Scotland. The same blessing was to be given to the 'Anglo-Normans' (as historians like to call the later Normans) in 1171 to invade Ireland, thus beginning centuries of oppression there too.

All this, we believe, is the just spiritual foundation that England lost in 1066, that ever since she has been seeking. However, she will not recover this foundation until she goes through a long and profound process of *Denomanisation*, of casting off all that has overlaid the beauty and the goodness and the truth of Old England and the Old English. And these, moreover, are the spiritual roots of England and Englishness.

Afterword: The Spirit of England

And did the Countenance Divine
Shine forth upon our clouded hills.
And was Jerusalem builded here
Among those dark Satanic mills.

William Blake

This Faith and Church that came from Jerusalem at the end of the sixth century lasted until the second half of the eleventh century, for nearly 500 years. It created the Saints and shaped a nation. That nation had a literature, an art, an architecture, learning and libraries. It possessed an educated noble class, a sense of unity. This England became therefore not just a location on a map, part of an island off the north-west coast of Europe, but rather a spiritual reality, Englishness. Her identity and essence, her soul or spiritual personality is her Saints. In this light England is a reality and an idea of eternal interest. Englishness is not a race or a skin colour but *values lived by, a Spirit.* And this is England's worth. These universal Christian values, are incarnate, made local and specific, in England, these values become *English values,* when borne by the Saints of England, whatever their background.

How then in these cosmopolitan times at the end of the Second Millennium do we square the realisation of Englishness, rooted in the First Millennium, with the rest of the world? Why is it important to hold on to the English values that we have uncovered?

We believe that it is because that without an appreciation of one's own native roots and culture, one cannot appreciate that of others. And in the Third Millennium, it will be vital to appreciate the roots and cultures of others, for we are sure to come into contact with them. Therefore we must first appreciate our own roots and culture, *radically* untangled from the Britannia mythology, from Confusion and Curse, *denominised.* With the yardstick of one's own culture rooted in the First Millennium, one can measure the roots and cultures of others in the Third Millennium.

This is not nationalism, the hatred of other countries, but patriotism, the love of one's country. Only a patriot can be an *interpatriot,* only one who loves his own country can love those of others. This is neither the ignorant bigotry of Little Englandism, nor the arrogant 'jingotry' of Great Britainism.

And this is why we may at times seem so fearful for the future. Cloaked by the deceiving name of 'harmony', tomorrow threatens sameness and uniformity and the death of the unique culture of Englishness. The English Soul and Faith, Englishness, was built up over five centuries and has survived as the underlying current of English culture in the face of all that the world has had to throw at it over the last thousand years. And today, although we may seem to be threatened from abroad, in fact we are threatened far more by our own indifference and faithlessness to the essential spiritual values of England, to the spiritual personality of England, to the English Soul, to the Spirit of England rooted in the First Millennium.

Those of us who do keep faith, believe also that the Spirit of England has survived not only through the Second Millennium on Earth, but also beyond history, beyond time and space, and that one day we shall meet all those who are the Spirit of England.

The Spirit of England comes from Jerusalem. This England, true England, remains faithful to the spirit and understanding, life and traditions of the Old Faith, planted among the English so long ago, by the Lord Himself through His Saints. Faithfulness to Her is faithfulness to national, patriotic tradition. Haunted by Her Saints, the Spirit of England worships the Living God and mystically belongs to the Commonwealth of all true Christian peoples. It was Her faithfulness to Christ which created a land of freedom and ordered living, the vestiges of which have lasted even until our own times. But this England is now retreated and hidden, in readiness for the Coming of Her Messiah.

And at that time, God's good time, the whole of the English Church shall gather. They shall come out of the North and the South, the East and the West. There shall go Archbishops, Bishops, Abbots, Abbesses, Her religious, and faithful clergy, and all the righteous people of God and their bright endeavours, all who have taken shelter beneath the broad and sacred raiment of Christ down all the ages. They have come out of the fiery trial, from weariness and want, to the Great and Everlasting Whitsun, the Bright Kingdom of the Spirit.

And this will be the first day of the Resurrection of England, of the Resurrection of the Spirit of England.

Fr Andrew Phillips
Seekings House
St Felix Tide 1999.

Nations, Nationalism and Nationalists

Tony Linsell

We live in an age when many English people, and in particular the young, know next to nothing about their history, and are uncertain about their national identity. One of the reasons for this sad state of affairs is that for many years the English have been encouraged to think of themselves as being primarily British and, more recently, as Europeans or even as *citizens of the world*; a term that reveals the confused thinking of those who use it. In schools, English history has been replaced by British and World history, and any promotion of an English national identity is treated as subversive of the state ideology. Those righteous individuals who promote the *official* creed are so convinced of its universal application and everlasting nature that they feel no need to defend it with rational argument. Instead, those unbelievers who openly question the assumptions that underlay it are depicted as heretics and fools.

To fully understand why Englishness is ridiculed and denied, it is necessary to step back from the fray in England and take a wider view of the forces that are intent on shaping our perceptions.

What is a Nation?

The word *nation* is commonly used in the following three ways:

1. As a synonym for *state*. For example, when the European Union is discussed, mention is often made of its member nations pooling and sharing their sovereignty. The members of the EU are in fact states.

2. As a term for the citizens of a state. For example, reference is often made to the British nation when what is meant is citizens of the UK or the British people. Also, at the time of the coming to power of Nelson Mandela there was much talk of the people of South Africa being one nation; a rainbow nation. What was meant was that the people of many nations shared the same citizenship.

3. As a term for a group of people who share a common descent, culture, history and language. For example, the Kurds, Zulus, Palestinians and Tibetans are all nations, as indeed are the English.

Those who are careless with their terminology, which includes many journalists, tend to use the words *state* and *nation* as if they are interchangeable. Those who study global society (International Relations) or are involved in inter-state relations have to be more precise with their terms and appreciate more the need to distinguish a state from a nation.

The misuse of the terms is mostly due to ignorance but sometimes it is done deliberately by ideologues who are wedded to the concept of an inclusive *civic-society* and believe that states should be central to the identity and loyalty of those who live in them. As a result, *nation* and *nationality* are used in a way that implies they are political rather than cultural terms. *Nationality* is equated with *citizenship*, a term that can be constitutionally defined. For example, if a person is a citizen of France they are deemed to be French and to owe loyalty to the French state.

A completely different view is that a nation is a community of people with a communal name, ancestry, culture, history and language. Those who take this stance believe that nations exist independently of states, and that nationality is determined by identification with and loyalty to a cultural entity; a nation. For example, an Algerian who becomes a French citizen remains an Algerian. It is this fundamental difference in outlook that is explored below.

It is widely recognised that it is very difficult to define a nation but that does not mean that nations do not exist. A fairly simple definition, or collection of guidelines, as to what constitutes a nation is that it is a group of people who share all or most of the following: a collective name; a perceived or real common ancestry; a history; a culture; a language; and sometimes a common religion. There is nearly always an association between a nation and a specific territory that is regarded as its homeland. A nation has myths, legends, heroes and loyalties. It is a community with a sense of solidarity and common identity; there is a *we* sentiment and a *they* sentiment; *insiders* and *outsiders*. A greater degree of empathy and sympathy exists among insiders than between insiders and outsiders. Indeed, the notion of *insiders* and *outsiders* derives from the concept of a community living closely together within a physical boundary, e.g. an encampment or settlement enclosed by a fence or ditch. A nation's boundary markers are more often cultural than physical.

One of the most important things that binds a nation together is the fact or perception of insiders sharing a common history and ancestry. The members of a nation usually have real ancestral links, but even in those instances where the links are weak, the illusion of common ancestry is possible because insiders share certain physical characteristics that make it possible for them to believe in a shared ancestry. As is so often the case, perception is more important than fact but pretence has its limits and it would be difficult, for example, for a Japanese to pretend to be a Zulu because whatever clothes the person wore or the language they spoke, their appearance would remain so different from that of Zulus that any claim to share a common ancestry would obviously be doubtful.

That we have mental images of Zulus, Swedes and Japanese indicates that the linked factors of common physical characteristics and common ancestry are important considerations in determining membership of national communities. Despite the instinctive links we make, some ideologues are outraged by the idea that common ancestry has any part in determining nationality, not because it is untrue but because it is ideologically inconvenient. The very people who deny a link between kinship and nationality when defining, for example, Swedish nationality, nevertheless think it relevant when, for example, determining membership of North American Indian nations. An instance of this is the procedure used when the US government granted the remnants of certain Indian nations various land rights in a belated attempt to compensate them for the loss of their homelands. The financial benefits for members of those nations can sometimes be great, and there are many claimants. The method used to establish membership of an Indian nation is ancestry, which has to be proved. In other words, that which determines membership of a North American Indian nation is judged to be *in the blood*. Place of residence or birth or the expression of a firmly held belief by the applicant that s/he is a member of the appropriate tribe/nation counts for little. A similar process is used by the US government for determining who are indigenous Hawaiians.

Other factors that help identify a nation are myths and folklore that throw light on its origins and ancestry. Mythology is important even when it is only loosely based on fact or is a complete invention, as is the case with the various legends of King Arthur.[1] Folklore and history help to unite a nation and give it a distinct identity but it need not be one hundred percent *true* in order to fulfil that function.

Individuals tend to feel more secure when they are in the company of persons with whom they have much in common; birds of a feather flock together. Common values, experiences, attitudes and perceptions help make up the glue that bind together both small, face to face, local communities and large national communities. A nation is organic; it lives; it is more than the sum of its parts; it repairs and renews itself; it has a memory; it evolves. Its personality is to be found in its culture, its institutions and the attitudes and behaviour of its parts. Each member of a nation is a link between its past and its future. As with all living things a nation has to renew itself if it is to survive. Each generation preserves and renews the national culture and adds to it so that it in turn becomes part of the nation's future and its past. When a nation ceases to renew itself it dies and the memory of those that have gone before and the culture they helped to weave dies with it: it is a loss to all mankind. A nation is a reference point for individuals, it is a community where individuals can feel comfortable and at ease. A nation provides physical and cultural surroundings that are familiar and unthreatening. A nation is a home, and for many individuals it is such an important part of their being that they are prepared to endure hardships and to fight and die in its defence.

---

[1] The invented tales of a King Arthur were promoted by the Normans in place of English history. It was part of a policy of that can be called cultural genocide. The aim was to impose on the English a history of Britain in which the English played little part except as villains. This fictional account served the dual purpose of providing the Britons with a glorious history that made them feel better about themselves, and undermined English national identity, thus making the English more accepting of Norman rule. The legends took on a life of their own and as they developed they came to represent an ideal of chivalrous behaviour which influenced real knights and kings.

Nations – Community and Communication

A nation is a community. One of the key elements of community is an exchange of information, hence, the level of communications technology available at any time or place is an important factor in determining the numerical and geographical size of communities. The dramatic improvements that have been made in travel and communication technology during the past two hundred years have enabled communities to become larger by making it possible for larger groups of people to be aware that they share common myths, memories, symbols, folklore, values and perceptions. Developments in engineering skills, scientific knowledge and political organization have all played a part in expanding the boundaries of community. Sailing ships, roads, bridges, printing, railways, the telephone, aircraft, television, satellites and computers, have contributed to faster and wider communications and have enabled individuals to be in physical, visual and intellectual contact with many more members of their own national community, and of other national communities.

One of the consequences of improved communication is that a sense of community is no longer as dependent as it once was on individuals being geographically close to one another in face to face relationships. Thus, the importance of local communities has generally lessened, while national communities have become more important in establishing identity and loyalties.[2]

The development of communications technology has not only enabled nations to grow in size and cohesion, but has also provided governing elites with the means to increase the power of the state and exercise control over ever larger numbers of people by means of increasingly sophisticated techniques of persuasion. In other words, those things that have made possible greater national cohesion have also enabled states to become more powerful.

Developments in technology and organization have made it possible for national communities to become wider and deeper but those factors did not create nations and nationalism. Nations and nationalism have existed for thousands of years and are not, as is sometimes suggested, products of the industrial revolution or capitalism, although those things have influenced the way nationalism has evolved. The sentiment itself is much the same as it has always been, but what has changed is the way governing elites have manipulated national loyalties so as to use them for the benefit of the state and elite interests. The Black African nations that are commonly called tribes, existed long before the advent of modern capitalism and industrialisation. A tribe such as the Ndebeli (Matabele), whose language is part of the Bantu group, meets the definition of a nation but it was not invented by intellectuals or conjured out of thin air by capitalists. It is the modern sub-Saharan <u>states</u> of Africa that were invented. European outsiders drew lines on maps with apparent disregard for national homelands and little

---

[2] It is sometimes argued that the Internet has led to the growth of new small communities spread over a wide geographical area. However, such groups are interest groups rather than communities because the common point of contact is typically limited to one area of interest or activity.

consideration for the interests of those living there. It is that history and the continuing denial of the importance of national boundaries (geographical, cultural and political) by the current governing elites of those states that is responsible for much of the turmoil in Africa. In states such as Uganda, the governing elite is engaged in what is called a policy of *nation building*. What they are really trying to do is weaken or destroy nations in order to create allegiance to a state. They face a difficult task because the communal instincts that bind nations together have evolved over millions of years and are deep within us; they will not evaporate in order to satisfy a preference for artificial political boundaries, over natural communal boundaries. It would be wiser to abandon the recently created state boundaries and instead, as far as is possible, map national boundaries. The creation of real nation-states would remove the wasteful and time-consuming distraction of internal national rivalries from domestic politics. A nation that has its own state is relatively well placed to enjoy the internal consensus and cohesion that is necessary if a nation is to effectively pursue its external interests.

Nations and States

During the 18th and 19th centuries capitalism and industrialisation greatly increased the power of states and made it possible for those who controlled them to mobilise more resources for the purpose of pursuing policy goals that were said to be in *the national interest*.[3] Governing elites set about identifying the interests of the nation with those of the state. The two quite distinct concepts were merged into one and the confusion it caused continues today. The purpose of that deliberate policy is the same now as it was then, to harness the communal strength of a nation and use it to pursue the interests of the state and those who control it. What is commonly seen as the rise of modern nationalism would be better viewed as the rise of modern statism.[4] Little has changed since then in as much as the state is still presented as the embodiment of the nation, and the loyalty that is instinctively given to the nation is still demanded by the state.

The tactic used to promote the preferred perception of a nation was to redefine *nation* in a way that stripped away all the inconvenient cultural attributes and made it into something that suited liberal political theory. Two commonly used 19th century definitions of a nation are given below.

> A nation is a grand solidarity constituted by the sentiments of sacrifices which one has made and those that one is disposed to make again. It supposes a past, it renews itself especially in the present by a tangible deed: the approval, the desire, clearly expressed, to continue the communal life. The existence of a nation is an everyday plebiscite.

> Ernest Renan, French historian, in *Qu'est-ce qu'une nation?* (1882)

---

[3] States rarely pursue the *national* interest. It is more usual for them to pursue *state* interests, which are usually the same as the interests of the state's governing elite.

[4] Statism is the theory or practise of centralising economic and political power in the state.

Ernest Renan's definition is one that is often quoted and is in many respects valid. However, its popularity among liberals is due to the fact that it describes a civic society and conveniently lacks any reference to kinship, language, history and a homeland.

Another definition, which is more easily recognised for what it is, comes from John Stuart Mill. Again, it gives a flavour of what constitutes a real nation and real nationalism but omits any mention of culture and a perceived common ancestry.

> A portion of mankind may be said to constitute a nationality if they are united among themselves by common sympathies which do not exist between them and any others – which make them co-operate with each other more willingly than with other people, desire to be under the same government, and desire that it should be government by themselves or a portion of themselves exclusively.

John Stuart Mill, *Considerations on Representative Government* (1861)

The increasing ability of states to mobilise resources (technological and human) and the congruence, more or less, of national and state boundaries, made it easier for the idea to gain hold that state and nation were the same thing. Where several nations were incorporated into one state (e.g. the UK) the governing elite set about creating a new *national* identity (e.g. the British nation) which is not a national identity but a civic identity.

In recent times, and especially since WWII, the interests of governing elites and the states they control have become even more remote from the interests of the nations they once claimed to represent. Indeed the distance is now so great that some governing elites no longer justify the existence of the state on the grounds that it pursues the interest of its core nation. Instead, they deny the relevance or even the existence of nations and see only civic societies and *civic nationalism*, which amounts to loyalty and devotion to the state. The existence of modern states, and our supposed obligation to obey their rules, has long been rationalised by an argument based on a clearly fictional account of a *natural state* and a binding *social contract* that we are all deemed to have entered into. According to this model, which attempts to make states and constitutions look part of the natural order, states are a collection of neutral institutions that arbitrate between the competing interests of their citizens. In return for providing that service, states are deemed able to command the loyalty of their citizens. To attempt to overthrow the state and its governing elite is treated as the worst of crimes (treason) and deserving of the most severe penalty (death).

The social contact justification for states completely ignores the fact that real nations are bound together by threads spun from kinship, culture and interests. It is true that nations have a political dimension but it is not the only one. Nationalists argue that the loyalty a community owes to its political institutions is conditional on those institutions pursuing the interests of the community, as determined by the community. And those communal interests include cultural interests.

Nationalists see states as merely a means to a communal end, but liberals see them as things that exist in their own right, apart from and above their individual citizens. Nationalists believe that each nation is best served by its own state, and that loyalty is only owed to a state if it is serving the interests of the nation. Liberals maintain that one state can serve many nations, and that all citizens owe loyalty to the state. This fundamental difference of view is central to the dislike that liberal-statists and liberal-globalists have for nations, nationalists and nationalism, and the reason for the campaign of vilification that has been directed against them for many years. Such has been the success of the campaign that *nationalist* is used as a term of abuse, and nationalism is equated with demonic forces.

That ideological onslaught has become more intense and wide-ranging in recent times due to the emergence of a global-elite that is detached from nations and has only a logistical interest in the preservation of states.[5] Like other elites, it has common interests, values, perceptions and goals. Unlike other elites it does not appeal to a national or state identity but to a global identity and promotes the fiction of a global village bound together by the non-sexist equivalent of a brotherhood of mankind. This naïve world-view, which is peddled by the global-elite, is different from that promoted by state elites but it serves the same purpose, which is to better enable it to pursue its own interests while claiming to be acting in pursuit of a noble ideal. Thus, the global-elite deploys military force and economic sanctions in the name of peace, democracy and human rights, and in accordance with the wishes of the *International Community*.

What some call the *International Community*, others call the *New World Order* or the *global-elite*. In order to discover what the term *International Community* actually means, those who use it should be asked the following questions. Who are the members of the International Community and who has the right to speak for it? How is it known what the wishes of the International Community are? Whose interests are being served? Is peace being used as an excuse for war? Is democracy being used as an excuse for tyranny? Are human rights being used as an excuse for effecting their denial? In short, what is the pay-off and for whom?

On close examination, the International Community will be seen to be a global-elite that has the roots of its power anchored in a relatively small group of very powerful states, corporations and institutions. It is through those agencies that elite power is exercised and its interests pursued. The wellbeing of nations plays no part whatsoever in the global-elite's assessment of its interests. In fact, it is openly hostile to the idea of nations because it sees a world containing many cultures, identities and loyalties as a hindrance to the worldwide acceptance of its value and perceptions. The global-elite

---

[5] States serve the function of raising taxes, providing basic services, keeping order and maintaining the politico-economic conditions favourable to a particular type of global economy.

wants to destroy and sweep away what it cannot use to its advantage. In the place of nations it is promoting new civic and institutional identities.

The global-elite realises that there is a limit to the elasticity of national loyalty, which has been stretched to near breaking point by states. In its place, the International Community is promoting loyalty to something far more distant and vague than a state; it is loyalty to a global society, a global culture, and a universal ideology. In return for supplying an abundance of goods and services, the global-elite demands acceptance of its values and perceptions and the right to root out or render ineffective those who reject them. Unsurprisingly, despite its immense power, it finds it difficult to compete with or destroy national loyalties, which are founded on considerations other than the need to maximise the consumption of goods and services.

Like all centralists, of whatever political hue, the global-elite prefers an atomised society of individuals who are powerless before the might of a relatively small co-ordinated ruling group. When national communities and their interests and loyalties persist, what better way to counter them than to create multi-nation states, denigrate national identity, and promote civic societies. To top it all, globalism is promoted as being both desirable and inevitable. The strategy employed is one of demoralising and thereby defeating an enemy by convincing it that it cannot win; the outcome is proclaimed to be inevitable; why stand in the way of *progress* and history?

In its effort to manipulate our communal instincts for the purpose of creating a communal global identity and making us see ourselves as citizens of the world, the global-elite is undermining the economic, political and military independence of the very states that provide the foundation for its power. The increasing unwillingness and inability of states to challenge *global forces* and *progress*, prevents them from performing their traditional functions, and undermines the liberal justification for the existence of states, which is that they arbitrate between the conflicting interests of their citizens, and defend those citizens and their civic society from outside forces. The waning of citizens' confidence in the ability of states to influence events is made worse by globalists who insist that states *as we know them* are no longer functional and need to be replaced by super-states, regional trading blocs, and global institutions that are able to enforce regulations which conform with the doctrine and needs of global liberalism.

It is difficult to understand why a national community or an individual citizen should be expected to be loyal to a political structure (a state) that has diminishing power and does not represent communal or individual interests? Even more difficult to understand is why a national community should be loyal to remote organizations that are even less concerned than states to pursue national interests? What role is there for a dying British state that is continually ceding powers to a newborn European state, the EU? Why should the English willingly sacrifice anything, especially their lives, to defend a structure like the EU, which is even less inclined than the UK to represent English communal interests or even recognise the English as a nation?[6]

Summary

Communities are exclusive in that membership is open only to those who meet informal and often indefinable conditions. All communities have boundary markers and all communities, be they nuclear families or nations, discriminate between insiders and outsiders. Even African, Asian and North American Indian nations discriminate because without discrimination there can be no boundaries and no community. Nations are not something that one can choose to join like a club. Membership is not open to all and sundry. Nationality is not a commodity, a fashion accessory or lifestyle that can be adopted and discarded at will.

The communal loyalties that naturally exist within a nation were first exploited for the benefit of states but now that some state elites have merged into a global-elite, it has been recognised that there is a limit to the extent to which communal instincts can be stretched and manipulated. The global-elite sometimes attempts to use communal instincts for the benefit of new elite institutions such as the EU and NATO but for the most part it is opposed to *community* and instead prefers *society*; the more atomised and individualistic the better. To that end it promotes the destruction of national cultures and identities, and in their place it promotes a global junk-culture which values individualism, image and immediate self-gratification; all of which are bound up with consumption and status. In place of cultural and ideological diversity, we are *given* cultural and ideological conformity. The individualism that is forced on us is that of sheep in a flock.

National communities, and the sub-communities within, are linked together by certain common cultural, physical, behavioural and perceptual characteristics that mark them off from other communities. If national communities are pushed aside in order to make way for multi-national civic societies and a citizen of the world identity, the communal glue will be lost and the grand new ideological creations will fracture and fall apart. They will be unable to satisfy the communal instincts that combine and encourage insiders to:

> *co-operate with each other more willingly than with other people, desire to be under the same government, and desire that it should be government by themselves or a portion of themselves exclusively.*

---

[6] The EU promotes a common European identity by various means including literature designed for distribution in schools. The emphasis tends to be on a supposed common Celtic and Christian heritage. It was recently suggested that the school history syllabus in England should place greater emphasis on Britain's Norman heritage and the link it provides to the continent. The thread running through all the EU identity propaganda is that nations and nationalism are problems that need to be overcome so that we can all live happily in peace and prosperity.

Nationality and Citizenship

Nationality

Nationality is the condition, or fact, of belonging to a body of people sharing a common descent, culture, history and language. Nationality is normally acquired at birth; individuals are normally born into a community. It is the <u>perception</u> of a common ancestry and shared communal experiences that binds a nation together.

At the heart of nationality is a feeling of belonging and oneness that marks out a communal boundary. There is a *we sentiment* and a *they sentiment*. Such sentiments are not, as many wish us to believe, evil and deserving of eradication. On the contrary, they are the sentiments that are at the heart of any community anywhere in the world, and give rise to positive communal thoughts and deeds. It is unfortunate that Europeans are encouraged to feel guilty about their communal instincts while others are encouraged to flaunt and celebrate them.

It is difficult to frame exact rules for determining who is a member of a given nation but a useful guide, which can be used for any nation, is as follows: I am English if I believe[7] that I am English <u>and</u> if I am accepted as being English by the members of that group of people who are commonly recognised as being English. It is a two-way instinctive relationship between individual and community. I could, for example, assert that I am Japanese but if I have physical and cultural characteristics that are not Japanese, as determined by the Japanese, I will not be accepted as part of the Japanese community. No amount of law making, sulking or haranguing will alter that.

The two-way process of selection for inclusion or exclusion helps provide an answer to the question often thrown at nationalists, "What does it mean [for example] to be English?" The aim of the questioner is to draw out a list of characteristics that identify the English. Those asked are usually stumped for an answer, which is not surprising because the process of inclusion and exclusion is not a conscious one and does not work in the way implied by the question. The English, like all other nations, first see characteristics that exclude people because that is a more efficient way of working when analysing vast amounts of information.[8] Most of the Earth's population can be quickly excluded from membership of any given nation on the basis of appearance and language. If necessary, other tests of varying degrees of sophistication can be used until we are satisfied that the person is either an *insider* or an *outsider*.

---

[7] The word 'believe' is used for the sake of brevity but it is hardly adequate to convey the emotional feeling of identity with and concern for a nation that is at the heart of nationality.

[8] It is usual when processing a large amount of information to set markers, and exclude information that falls outside the set boundaries. Alan Turin applied this principle when devising the system known as the Bombe, which automated and speeded up the daily processing of information for the purpose of breaking the German Enigma code during World War II.

If the person is accepted as an insider, the instinctive assessment process goes on and makes other judgements about the person, including such things as their social class. At this *insider* level of assessment, the filtering process can make finer distinctions because we have far more experience of dealing with insiders and can make better use of small amounts of information. For example, if a Russian gives me his home address it will tell me little, if anything, about him because my knowledge of Russia and things Russian is poor. An address in my home town will tell me far more about the person who lives there.

Nationality is a total experience that starts in the family, which is the smallest community. Children are born into both a family and the linked wider communities of which that family is part. They are immersed in and soak up like a sponge the language, culture and history of those communities.[9] That experience helps mould children and give them an identity and sense of belonging. They pick up habits of behaviour and thought that are part of what is meant by national character. That character building process, if that is what it can properly be called, works best when there is cultural immersion and socialisation from a very early age. Once a national identity has been absorbed, it is embedded for life. It shapes values and perceptions in a way that makes it impossible for a member of one nation to completely shake off that identity and take on another. Learning another nation's customs, history and language is not enough because the new information is laid on old foundations.

The link between kinship, identity and loyalty can be illustrated as follows. An adopted child reared from a baby by loving adopted parents is likely to feel love and affection for those parents. When the child learns of its adoption it will normally want to seek out its biological parents. If they are found, the child is likely to feel an attachment to them that is different from that felt for the adopted parents, who it will probably continue to love as before. This need to know our origins is instinctive and essential to our sense of identity and belonging. It is therefore understandable that when a child learns that its real parents belong to a nation different from the one it has been raised in, it is likely to be drawn to that other nation's culture, and identify with it. This can cause difficulties, which are made worse when differences of race are added to those of nationality. The experience of many children involved in cross-race adoptions is one of confusion in adulthood due to conflicting communal identities and loyalties. Having been immersed in one culture from birth and having had that identity imprinted on

---

[9] Young children naturally absorb cultural information from those around them. This instinct enables them to learn up-to-date survival strategies that can be laid over their long-term survival instincts. This ability to quickly adapt to the immediate environment has evolved over millions of years, and under conditions where the 'cultural' information absorbed helped individuals and communities to survive and reproduce. We now have conditions where children are subject to the influence of agencies that promote values and perceptions which are harmful to both individual and communal survival and reproduction. The result is a high proportion of young adults with attitudes and behavioural habits that make them well suited for life in the virtual-reality world promoted by the global junk-culture but ill-equipped for survival in the real world. Natural selection ruthlessly weeds out those with unsuitable survival strategies.

them they find it difficult, if not impossible, to feel totally part of another culture to which they are subsequently drawn. They cannot overcome the fact that the first all-important immersion in a communal identity is a one-off experience.

In a similar way, children with parents of the same race but different nationality have to deal with conflicting attractions and loyalties. However, the problem is usually not so great for them because they are generally drawn to, and accepted by, at least one of the nations to which they are linked by kinship. A child raised in the national homeland, culture and language of one parent is likely to be drawn to that nation and be accepted by it. However, physical appearance and language skills can sometimes play a more important part than upbringing in determining which community a person is drawn to and which community accepts them. If a person's physical or cultural characteristics differ greatly from the norm for a particular nation, that person is unlikely to seek acceptance in it or to be accepted by it.

Liberals feel the need to put a positive slant on these things and suggest that children with parents of different nationality or race have the advantage of two identities and two cultures.[10] But is it really possible to immerse oneself in two cultures, identify with two histories, feel an insider in two communities, and, more difficult still, be accepted as a full member of two communities? The answer is probably, no. To feel an insider and be accepted as an insider it is usually necessary for an individual to be immersed in the culture of that community from birth and to be free of traits that would cause the person to be seen as an outsider.

A nation is an extended family, and like a family it has a life greater than that of any single member. Nations, like families, are bound together by the bonds of empathy and loyalty that come from a shared identity. Those bonds are not just with the living but also with those who have gone before and those who are yet to come. That link is, in part, a culture one that is constantly evolving but which contains within it values and perceptions that endure from one generation to the next. This bonding within and between generations is not something that can be learned or feigned.

Summary

A group of persons are likely to form a nation if they share: a communal name; live in a territory that bears that name; share a common culture; ancestry; language; political institutions.

A nation is an extended community whose members share a complex web of relationships, perceptions and emotions. Membership does not depend on meeting conditions on a formal checklist. Kinship, language, history and culture are all factors that help determine who belongs to which nation but there is no system of

---

[10] Multiculturalism is an ideology (a very recent one) and should be subject to the same tests as any other. It is not, as many of its followers believe, derived from an unchallengable universal truth.

measurement that can be applied to them. Many of the 'flags' or 'markers' that we use to distinguish insiders from outsiders are noted subconsciously and the decisions are made instinctively. Insiders are able to recognise each other in informal ways that vary according to the needs of the time. To ask someone to describe the process by which they decide who is and is not a member of their nation is similar to asking a group of friends to explain how they decide who is and who is not a friend. It is not something we consciously think about and it is not something that is easy to describe. It is a process that is guided by a bundle of instincts that are deep within all of us and which cannot be eliminated by ideological conditioning, even though there are some who wish it were so.

Citizenship

Using *nationality* as a synonym for *citizenship* can cause confusion and misunderstanding. Nationality denotes membership of a particular community, while citizenship denotes membership of a civic-society. The two identities are sometimes complementary (in nation-states) and sometimes they conflict or have no close association (in multi-nation states).

A civic identity is like a national identity in that it is usually acquired at birth with no opportunity available for opting out or negotiating terms. Those born in the Soviet Union usually acquired Soviet citizenship and, like other Soviet citizens, became a part of Soviet society and were subject to the rules of the Soviet state, which like other states deemed that it had the right to demand obedience and loyalty in certain things. Soviet citizens also belonged to a nation (e.g. Russian, Latvian, Armenian) and a family, both of which are communities that endure despite the coming and going of states. In a similar way, a British citizen (more properly called a British subject)[11] might be English, Scottish, Welsh, Nigerian, Bangladeshi, Jamaican, Italian or a member of any nation you care to mention.[12] Citizenship indicates a person's relationship with a state (political structure) and is usually defined in a legalistic form of words that is embodied in the state's constitution. Nationality indicates a person's relationship with a nation (community and its culture) and cannot be formally defined.

Each state determines who its citizens are and how non-citizens can qualify for citizenship. The acquisition of citizenship is a legal formality that gives an individual civic rights and obligations. It is a legal procedure and because of that it is possible to

---

[11] A subject is a person who lives under (is subject to) the rule of a monarch. The term is technically correct but will cease to be so if the UK is absorbed into the European Union. *Subject* is probably no longer appropriate in the UK because although the monarch is Head of State he or she does not rule in any real sense and, in effect, acts as an unelected president. *Citizen* is the more appropriate term and also the more convenient to use.

[12] British subjects in the province of Northern Ireland who are Republicans or members of the 'Nationalist Community', consider themselves to be Irish. The position of the 'Loyalist Community' is more complex but they can, with justification, claim to be a nation with a homeland called Ulster. They are Ulstermen. Protestant describes their religion and Loyalist a political stance.

be a citizen of two or more states and have dual citizenship, which is often inaccurately termed, dual-nationality. Some states permit their citizens to hold dual citizenship but others do not.

Nationalists and Nationalism

Those who confuse *nation* with *state* get into difficulties when they come to use and define the words *nationalism* and *nationalist*. A definition of nationalism which suggested that it is *loyalty or devotion to one's state* clearly conflicts with reality because, for example, Kurds living in Turkey, Iraq and Iran are citizens of those states but they do not feel loyalty and devotion to them. Kurdish nationalists feel loyalty and devotion to the Kurdish nation, which has no state of its own. The existence of a Kurdish nation, Kurdish nationalism, and Kurdish nationalists are therefore not dependent upon there being a Kurdish state. Scottish nationalists provide an example of those whose loyalty and identity is with a nation in the proper sense of the word, and not with the state (UK) of which they are citizens. Nationalism precedes and gives rise to the demand for a state.

Nationalists

Nationalists are concerned for the wellbeing of their nation. The vast majority of people feel an instinctive attachment to a nation and are concerned to see it survive and prosper. In that sense most people are nationalists. Beyond that there are those who give political expression to their feelings and are commonly labelled as nationalists, either by themselves or others. Nationalists see nations and national identity as central to their political thinking and outlook on life. Gender, class and race are all secondary considerations because nationality encompasses all of those things. For a nationalist, nationality is the widest communal identity, and the one that is central to any valid claim for the right to self-government. The primary concerns of nationalists are the attainment or preservation of national unity, national identity, national independence, national self-government and the general wellbeing of their nation. A nationalist need not be of any particular political persuasion.

National communities evolve as they wind their way across the landscape of history. Their flow is sometimes hidden beneath the surface of events but all the while they are adapting and evolving so that when the nation re-emerges into the light it appears to outsiders as something new and different. It is often suggested that nationalists invent or reinvent nations but there is no magic formula that can make a nation from nothing. Nationalist intellectuals can help make nations visible but if they are to be effective in reawakening an outward expression and assertion of nationhood they need to tap into real, but often submerged, national identities, sentiments and loyalties. Their task is to reveal the threads of national identity in a way that meets the needs of the time. If a revivalist nationalist is proclaiming a bogus sense of nationhood, he or she will fail to achieve the aim because it is not possible to create a nation out of thin air.

Some nationalists and nationalisms are seen as more threatening than others to the dogma of the governing elite. One of the main reasons for hostility to English nationalism is that its opponents believe that if the English develop and express a strong national identity they will drop their British identity; Britishness will then be dead. That will create the problem of finding an identity for the non-English population of England. It will also remove the glue that holds the Union together, and the UK will fall apart. That process of disintegration will speed up when it eventually dawns on the English that the distribution of UK government resources greatly favours Scotland, Wales and Northern Ireland. The end of the Union in its present form will then be increasingly seen as a good thing, not least because it will free England from the financial burden of keeping the UK together. It follows that the various parts of the British governing elite have a common interest in maintaining the illusion of Britishness and of denigrating English nationalism. They do that by using phrases such as the sinister *dark forces of English nationalism* and the insulting *Little Englander*. Irish, Scottish and Welsh nationalists are treated far more kindly.

The Welshman, R. S. Thomas, reveals, in his concern to preserve Welsh culture and identity, much of what motivates and drives a nationalist. English liberals find him acceptable and patronise him because he is an elderly Welsh poet, and Welsh nationalism is not seen as a threat. R. S. Thomas is regarded as a *character* with romantic notions about a dying culture. His words are quoted, almost with affection, by liberals who would condemn him if he were English. He has said, "To me the average Englishman is a nationalist and England comes first. I'm not against this. When I am questioned I say I love Wales and I hope you love England. But in any free-for-all people are going to fight for their own country. So any Englishman worth his salt wants to keep England together. We know that the UK is only a euphemism for England. The Scots, the Irish, the Welsh are just appendages." He believes that a Welsh Assembly is better than nothing, despite being inspired by English imperialism rather than concern for Welsh rights.[13] He is greatly saddened by the colonisation of

---

[13] This is not altogether true because the Welsh Assembly was promoted by a predominantly Scottish Labour government. It made provision for a Scottish parliament and felt it necessary to offer the Welsh an assembly in an attempt to show that the constitutional arrangements had not been devised solely for the benefit of Scots or for the purpose of protecting the position of the Labour Party in Scotland. Devolution is clearly a device to cut the ground from beneath the Scottish National Party and its demand for independence. Instead of following the logic of devolution through and creating an English parliament, the government has set in motion a process of administrative change aimed at weakening England by dismembering it into nine regions. Such an outcome will rid the Scots of a powerful southern neighbour and prevent effective opposition to the unfair system that gives them a disproportionately large allocation of central government funds. That all this can be done without consulting the people of England and giving them the same opportunity as other parts of the UK to determine their own constitutional future, shows the contempt the governing elite have for the English.

Regions also serve the interests of the European Union, the power of which will increase with the weakening of the larger nations and member states. The EU policy of encouraging regionalism is necessary because the creation of a long-lasting European state will require the creation of a European identity among its citizens. To that end there is an attempt to replace national and state identities with regional and European identities. Sometimes it is convenient for the EU to use the nationalism of small

Wales by the English and his belief that only 22 percent of Wales remains Welsh. He would like Wales to have complete independence so that the Welsh have the power to determine their own affairs. He looks with envy at the Irish free state when he sees its flag flying and is greatly saddened by the materialism of many Welsh people who would rather enjoy a monetary advantage than enjoy the freedom to govern themselves. Thomas's frustration is such that he wishes the Welsh would rise in armed resistance and fight for their independence but he fears that it is too late and the Welsh will never be free.[14]

R. S. Thomas is in his eighties but has more fire in him than most of his countrymen, many of whom know little about their history, are unaware of the frailty of their culture and apathetic about the future of their nation. If sport and soap operas are available on television, and supermarkets open at convenient times, what need is there of a national culture and identity? The situation is even worse in England where watching and consuming help keep most of the population docile.

Fellow nationalists of whatever nation can understand the sadness and frustration that R. S. Thomas feels at the willingness of his countrymen to trade their culture and independence for strings of beads. His burning desire to protect and regenerate his nation is to be found in the hearts of nationalists everywhere.

Nationalism

Nationalism is loyalty or devotion to one's nation, and a desire for national self-government, which in the modern world can only be obtained through the creation of a state. Where a nation does not enjoy self-government, nationalism often expresses itself in the form of a political campaign (by nationalists) to achieve that end. The Kurds want to establish a state so that they can govern themselves and better protect their way of life. In other words they seek the self-determination that is deemed the right of *a people* by the UN Charter, Article 1(1). On establishing a state, Kurds will be able to engage in formal inter-state relationships for the purpose of pursuing their national interests. For example, they will be able to enter into treaty obligations, trade agreements and military and economic alliances. The creation of real nation-states greatly increases the likelihood of national interests and state interests coinciding.

Nationalism is a natural, healthy, inborn, tenacious communal sentiment, the expression of which is sometimes suppressed or buried before flowering again in unexpected ways. Nationalism is a sentiment based on common cultural characteristics, customs, traditions, ancestry, history, values and perceptions. It is an emotion that

---

nations to promote regional policy but that is felt to be a price worth paying if it leads to the weakening or break-up of large member states. The aim of the EU political elite is to create a civic-society in which no part is able to challenge the central governing authority. EU institutions will then justify their existence by claiming to be neutral arbiters in disputes between citizens and between regions.

[14] These sentiments were expressed in an article by Louise Jury published in *The Independent on Sunday*, 14th September 1997.

binds a large community together in a way that improves its opportunities for survival, security and cultural achievements. Nationalism is the soul of a community; a force that gives it shape and an identity. Nationalism is an instinct and an emotion; it is like love in that it has to be experienced before there can be any real understanding of it. It is not something that can be reduced to a formula or understood by academics probing it from the outside as if it were a laboratory specimen. No two samples are alike and each is constantly evolving. If academics of the ideological establishment were to escape from their dogmatic straitjacket and look within themselves, they would find a better understanding of the thing they are studying. Nationalism is energy and movement; it is constantly changing and never takes the same shape twice. It appears before each observer in a different form and the values and expectations of the observer colour the observations made. This explains why, with a few notable exceptions, the vast majority of an ever-increasing literature from the ideological establishment on the subject of nationalism treats it in a wholly unsympathetic and hostile manner. The common lines of attack are to dismiss nationalism as an irrelevant relic of a bygone age or to portray it as a dangerous state of mind found among those who are inadequate or evil. But what other response could realistically be expected of them?

Nationalism is not a passive sentiment, it is a communal sentiment that draws people together in an active defence of their collective sovereignty, culture and identity. All nationalisms are brewed from similar ingredients but each nation has a unique recipe that is constantly evolving in response to the needs of the time. This process of adaptation and evolution does not mean that the communal sentiment changes, it is just expressed in different ways in different times. When this is understood, it can be seen that there is little point in making a close examination of a particular nationalism at one time and then declaring it to be invented because it differs from an earlier expression of nationalism by the same group of people. Even more absurd is the suggestion that *nations* and *nationalism* only came into existence with the first use of those words. The English word *folk* (O.E. *folc*) is an excellent alternative to *nation* and better conveys its essence.

Three levels of Nation and Nationalism

Nationalism consists of many layers of sentiment, each of which merges with and is inseparable from the other layers. Despite the mingling, it is possible to detect three broad levels, each of which has its roots in different types of communal experience.

Level One – Day-to-Day Living

The first level is the physical one of place and kinship, and the instincts that are attached to them. This is the world of reproduction, families, territory and landscape; it is where the physical environment shapes the way kindred groups go about acquiring the necessities of life, such as food, water and shelter. It also plays a part in determining how those assets are shared and how the community defends its territorial boundaries.

A traditional face-to-face community is one where its members live close together in a manner that, on the whole, benefits them all by satisfying basic needs such as food, shelter, defence, and the opportunity for reproduction. Improvements over the years in communications technology has altered the meaning of *living closely together* and has enabled communities to exist where members have little if any direct face-to-face contact. The problem with relying on some types of sophisticated communication is that it can be used by those who own and manage it to shape the way a community sees itself or, if the communal identity is ignored, does not see itself. For example, in the UK, the broadcasting media, which is the most powerful medium for shaping perceptions of community and identity, promotes the values and perceptions of a governing elite that favours civic identity over national identity. Hence, Isaac Newton, William Shakespeare, Charles Darwin, and many others, cease to be English and are labelled (rebadged) British. When in certain situations Englishness cannot be ignored, and the institutionalised hostility to it has to be overcome, it is presented as an inclusive identity; if you live in England you are deemed to be English, unless of course you are Irish, Scottish or Welsh.

When the communications web of a widespread community becomes dependent upon institutions that are actively undermining communal ties and identity, the web becomes weak, broken and patchy. It is the task of nationalists to repair the web, either by ensuring that communal needs are served by existing institutions, or by making new pathways that bypass them. Nationalists need only bring the broken threads together to spark a spontaneous regeneration of communal identity, solidarity, and empathy.

Level Two – Culture

All communities have to solve similar problems but they do so in different ways according to their experience, resources and environment. The different circumstances and solutions give rise to different cultures, each of which is a store of knowledge that succeeding generations add to and pass on to the next. Cultures are blueprints for survival; some are more sophisticated than others but all are successful if they enable a community to adapt to its physical and social environment, and continually regenerate itself.

Nations exist in the minds of insiders and outsiders. Each nation is a unique mix of shared values and perceptions, of accumulated knowledge, experience and achievement expressed in such everyday things as what is eaten and how it is cooked. Architecture, crafts, art, myths, literature, music, dance, and much more, are part of a culture and give expression to it. Thus, the second level of community is a world of custom, culture, religion, law, science and all the things that spring from communal relationships and the struggle for survival. In all of these areas there are communal and cultural boundary markers that are instinctively recognised by insiders but are mostly invisible to outsiders who can see only the broad outline. Insiders and outsiders know that a community exists but neither are able to define its boundaries. Thus the question, what does it mean to be English or Irish or French, has no adequate answer.

Some nations have a strong culture and communal identity that enables them to survive periods of misfortune and decline. After the loss of their state and their homeland they appear to outsiders to be dead and gone forever, but then, after many generations they emerge in an evolved and invigorated form. Other nations, in similar circumstances, collapse and perish because they are either too small to sustain their way of life or their culture has become so diluted that they are unable to maintain communal boundaries.

Level Three – Imagination

If a nation is to survive territorial invasion, the loss of self-government, and a campaign of cultural genocide, it is essential that it inhabits a communal world of the imagination. This third level of community is one that outsiders can never see or gain access to; it is a communal virtual reality in which every member of a nation, past, present and future is linked. The physical deaths of those who have gone before do not prevent them from inspiring and motivating those who come after them. Offa, Alfred, Athelstan and Hereward are some of the big names from the distant past that live on in the web that is the communal memory and imagination of the English nation. There are also the many smaller names of individuals who have contributed something special to English culture and identity. Last but not least is the influence of all those who in having children and living their ordinary lives have played their part in keeping the communal identity alive and passing it from one generation to the next.

The world of the imagination is one of empathy, identity, loyalty and emotion. It is here that individuals are able to see beyond their immediate physical world and appreciate that they are, and will continue to be, part of something that has a life far larger than their own. This wider vision is at the heart of freedom because it takes us beyond our solitary human life and releases us from the constraints of time and space; it gives each of us a larger identity and a greater willingness to face hardship, danger and death.

Outsiders may share a nation's physical environment (homeland) and even go out of their way to adopt its customs and culture but they will never be able to enter the world of another nation's imagination because it is impossible for them to escape their own communal identity, which is moulded by their ancestry, upbringing and communal experiences. We carry with us through life the mark of the community into which we are born.

It is possible to chart some of the physical and cultural boundary markers of a nation but it is not possible to map mental boundary markers, which is why they are not only difficult to find but impossible to cross. Thus, the boundaries that exist in the communal mind are easier to defend than territory, provided of course there is the resolve to do so. It is for political nationalists to maintain that resolve by defending the national culture (e.g. history and language) and promoting a way of life that complements the communal instincts to reproduce and survive.

Political Nationalism

Nations usually identify with a particular territory; their homeland. Political nationalism is the force that strives to defend or create the conditions whereby the members of a nation are able to exercise their sovereign powers through their own political institutions (a state) within the secure boundaries of their homeland. The underlying assumption is that the greatest freedom and security for a nation is to be found when the nation has its own state (nation-state) which it manages and defends. For example, Japan is the homeland of the Japanese, and the Japanese believe that the territory is theirs and that they have the right to defend it and live in it according to their customs. They have the right to govern themselves within that territory in any way they choose, and they have the right to determine who enters their country and on what conditions. They make their own laws, police their own country, and dispense their own justice. Nationalists recognise that all nations have those rights and that pursuing them is a proper expression of nationalism.

Political nationalism has a side to it that is often ignored, which is the belief that self-governing communities provide the secure and free environment in which democracy can best flourish and individuals fulfil their potential. Communal freedom creates the conditions for individual freedom, contentment, and happiness. It produces rounded people with a sense of identity and a feeling of belonging that helps them fully develop and bloom. Individual freedom outside of a community tends to be selfish and lead to conflict because there are no communally agreed and enforced limits to the expression of that freedom. Community provides a channel for the expression of individual freedom, and enables it to flourish in a way that benefits both the individual and the community.

The best environment for a democratic civic-society is one where citizens share a wide range of common values and perceptions. In other words, where there is congruence between cultural community and political society.[15] A political society that includes two or more communities with separate cultural identities, histories and values will fracture along communal fault lines. The result will be either the domination of one group over others or a power-sharing arrangement that undermines the ideal of a civic-society in which citizens behave and vote as individuals rather than as members of competing communities.

---

[15] The American Constitution was written for just that sort of homogeneous community, which perhaps explains why it is unsuited to the divided political and cultural society that the US has become.

One of the consequences of bringing people with very different cultural values and perceptions together in one political society is that it stimulates defensive communal instincts. Communal competition and conflict leads to communal insecurity and pressure for greater internal conformity, which in turn leads to a reduction in the scope for personal choice, not an increase. This can often be seen when the members of one nation settle in another nation's homeland. The settler community is usually more conservative and less tolerant of 'deviant' social/cultural behaviour than it would have otherwise been because, if it is to survive, it has to work harder to maintain its boundaries and its identity.

In addition to the internal pressures that limit personal freedom, there are the external pressures brought by other communities when they are offended by certain types of behaviour. What is an individual to do if the behaviour deemed offensive to other communities is thought acceptable, or even desirable, by his own community? If the personal freedom of individuals is restrained not only by the norms of their community but also by the norms of other communities, there is less individual freedom than there might otherwise be.

The behaviour of others is usually not a problem for those who have no experience of it in their everyday life. Such a happy position is enjoyed by nations that have their own state (nation-state) and are able to live as they wish without pressure from outsiders to change their ways.

Early English National Identity

Before the English (Engle) came to Britain they lived in the Jutland peninsular and their homeland was called Angeln. During the 1st century, Tacitus recorded the existence of a tribe, which in Latin he called the Anglii.[16] It was one of seven tribes, safe behind defences of rivers and forests, who worshipped Nerthus, Mother Earth. The next we learn of the early English is from the Old English poem, *Widsið*, which tells us of the first King Offa, king of the English. After naming thirty-three kings the poem goes on:

> Offa rules Angeln, Alewih the Danes
> – he was the bravest of all –
> yet he did not better Offa in heroic feats
> for of these men Offa, while still a boy,
> won the greater kingdom.
> In his time no other won greater fame
> in battle. With his lone sword
> he fixed the border with the Myrgings
> at Fifeldor. Since then the
> English and the Swabians have kept it as Offa made it.[17]

---

[16] The early name of the English was *Angel* but Roman writers such as Tacitus used the Latinised name *Anglii* which later became *Angle*. In English *Angel* evolved into *Engle* and then into *Englisc* and *English*. In Old English *sc* is pronounced *sh*.

[17] There are two versions of the story. Background information in *English Heroic Legends* by Kathleen Herbert.

During the century following Offa's death the English crossed the North Sea to Britain and conquered and settled large tracts of land. The migration was so complete that by the time it was finished the old country of Angeln (England) stood empty.[18] The many small kingdoms the English established in Britain gradually merged into several larger ones which are known today as Northumberland (*Norðhymbre* – land north of the River Humber), Mercia (*Mercie* – the frontier lands – central England and the area to its west), and East Anglia (*Eastengle*). To the south, warriors and settlers from the federation of tribes known as the Saxons (*Seaxe*) conquered and settled the lands that came to be known as Essex, Sussex, Wessex, and Middlesex (*Eastseaxe* – East Saxons, *Suð Seaxe* – South Saxons, *West Seaxe* – West Saxons, and *Middelseaxan* – Middle Saxons[19]). There were also Jutes (Kent and the Isle of Wight) and Frisians, a people much involved in trade who seem to have settled in towns and near ports throughout the land.

After many generations, the Anglo-Saxons (*Engle-Seaxe*) began to think of themselves as one nation. They were able to merge into one national community because their appearance, language, mythology and way of life were very similar. In all those respects they differed from the Welsh who were regarded as foreigners. Looks and language where then, as now, generally the easiest and quickest ways of telling an insider from an outsider. Language is a particularly important boundary marker because it is shaped by and reflects the values, history, geographical location, world-view, and everyday life of those to whom it belongs.[20]

Like other nations, the English in Britain were defined by what they had in common with other *insiders* and how they differed from *outsiders* with whom they came into contact. The high level of cultural and linguistic unity among the North Sea Germanic tribes that migrated to Britain was strengthened by the political unity which grew out of the custom of recognising one of their kings as an over-lord or Bretwalder.[21] The gradual merging together of Engle, Saxon, Jute and Frisian communities did not destroy local loyalties. The men of Wessex and Mercia fought as Englishman and as West Saxons and Mercians when, under King Æthelstan and his brother Edmund, they defeated a combined force of Norsemen and Scots at the Battle of Brunanburh in the 10th century.[22]

---

[18] Bede's, *Ecclesiastical History of the English People*.

[19] There is no evidence for an early Middle Saxon kingdom and it is probable that the name was given to the territory west of, and including London, long after the Anglo-Saxon conquest and settlement had taken place.

[20] For that reason Esperanto, an artificial language, is unlikely to ever amount to much. It is not part of a national culture and is sterile despite the attempts of some of its supporters to breathe life into it and give it a soul.

[21] Bretwalder perhaps means *Britain ruler* or *sole ruler*.

[22] For details of the battle see the Old English verse, *The Battle of Brunanburh*.

The merging of peripheral identities into the core English identity gathered pace during the 9th century, when Danish raids on England grew in frequency, size and duration until they amounted to an invasion before which all of the English kingdoms fell one by one.[23] Alfred became king of Wessex upon the death of his brother in 871. After several battles with the Danes, Alfred paid them tribute and managed to secure peace for a short period. In January 878 Alfred was defeated by the Danes at Chippenham. He took refuge at Athelney, in the Somerset marshes, from where he organised the formation of a new army.

Alfred emerged from hiding in May 878 and successfully lead the English against the Danes at Edington. That was followed by a series of battles and agreements that enabled the English to first recover Wessex then much of Mercia. The coming together of men from many parts of England to fight against a common enemy increased the sense of unity and national identity. Alfred assisted that process in many ways, including the promotion of English as a language of record. He also created a system of national defence in depth based on burhs (fortified towns) that enabled him to fight successful military campaigns and create the foundations of a well organized state.

About the year 886[24] Alfred and the Dane, Guthrum, entered into a treaty which divided England along a line running roughly from Chester to Bedford to London. King Alfred was recognized as overlord of the territory to the south and west and Guthrum ruled that part of England that lay to the north and east.[25] The Treaty protected the interests of Englanders living in the Danelaw by ensuring that they enjoyed the same compensation rights as Danes of equal social rank. Danes living in Alfred's kingdom enjoyed reciprocal rights. The arrangement demonstrates that Alfred did not believe that all within his kingdom were English, and it supports the view that Englishness, then as now, was determined by ancestry, culture and loyalties; not by place of birth or residence. That view is unacceptable to the modern-day ideologues who are eager to project their civic-society and an inclusive English identity back into a rewritten history. They are uncomfortable with the idea that all who lived in Alfred's kingdom were his subjects but not all were English.

Alfred set about building an English nation-state and in doing so he gave hope to the English that they and England would one day be united under an English king, which

---

The organization of English soldiers into regiments recruited from districts continues today and is said to foster a greater sense of comradeship, community and resolve than is evident among soldiers who have no regional or communal ties.

[23] *Viking* from Old English *wicing* meaning *sea pirate*. It is probable that *viking* was not used in the modern sense until the 19th century when it was applied to all 9th–11th century Scandinavian invaders in much the same way that the term Saxon had been used for the Germanic North Sea tribes. To refer to all Scandinavians of that time as vikings is to suggest a uniformity in culture, allegiance and purpose that did not exist.

[24] The date is uncertain. See Alfred P. Smyth, *King Alfred the Great*, OUP, 1995, p. 92.

[25] The Danelaw was the territory in which the law of the Danes was applied.

they were. Alfred was an English nationalist who acted in the interests of all the English whether they were in his kingdom or that of the Dane, Guthrum. In showing concern for the interests of those of his countrymen who were not and had never been his subjects, he demonstrated a sense of identification with and empathy for them that is indicative of nationalism and a community of the imagination. The English Chronicle (Anglo-Saxon Chronicle) records that a treaty with Guthrum and all the people of East Anglia was concluded by *King Alfred and the councillors of all the English nation*. The entry for the year 900 records the death of Alfred (in 899) and states that he was *king over all the English, except for that part which was under Danish rule*. In other words, the English, who formed by far the greater part of the population ruled by the Dane Guthrum, continued to be recognised by both sides as English. That population provided the core culture and identity into which the Danes where absorbed.

Alfred strengthened all the elements of national identity. In addition to updating the Law Codes and putting in place a network of burhs, he also encouraged the creation of centres of learning, and was responsible for the writing of an English history that was regularly added to for the next 200 years. He translated, or had translated, many texts, religious and secular, from Latin into English. The measures that Alfred took to defend, strengthen and preserve the English nation, its culture and way of life, where such that he deserves to be remembered as a great Englishman.[26]

It is a cause for sadness that in our time the English are for the most part unaware of Alfred's achievements or even of his existence. Those modern day institutions that should be passing on English history to English children seem to believe that Alfred is irrelevant to contemporary life. He is not an icon for those who wish to denigrate and deny Englishness.

The English of Alfred's time would view with dismay and disbelief the English of today, so many of whom are timid and apologetic about their history and ignorant of the deeds of their ancestors. Fortunately, there are still English men and women who carry within them the courage and energy of their forebears.

Afterword

Nationalism is the name given to a natural sentiment that is essential to the wellbeing of all communities. It is entirely natural and healthy for individuals to act together for the purpose of keeping alive their communal identity and imagination. That does not

---

[26] It can be argued that Alfred, through his support of the Church, assisted the import into England of an alien Mediterranean culture and religion that weakened an essentially North European English culture. However, that process had been under way for nearly three hundred years, with the result that most of the governing elite was under the influence of a foreign power (the Church) and used a foreign language (Latin) for the business of the kingdom (state). As with the later but bloodier arrival of the Normans and their Norman-French language, the English survived as a nation. Alfred in effect Anglicised the Church and used it to strengthen an English identity. He borrowed and made English those things that he believed were useful.

mean that they are filled with a fear and hatred of outsiders or wish to harm them. The assertion of national identity is not an act of aggression and it does not imply a belief that one culture or way of life is superior to another. Neither does it imply that the members of one community are superior or inferior to others. What it does mean is that the members of all national communities have an interest in their communal achievements and shared experiences because those achievements and experiences have helped to shape them as individuals and as a group. The English, like all other nations, naturally have an emotional as well as an intellectual interest in their communal history because it uncovers the beginnings of a fascinating journey they have travelled together; it reveals the roots of their Englishness.

It is unfortunate, to put it mildly, that those who control the institutions of the state should see it as entirely natural and healthy for other nations to take an interest and pride in their national (ethnic) identity, but think it a perversion when the English do the same. The reason is plain to see; the English are an ideological inconvenience, and because of that they are either ignored or made to bear the scoffing of fellow English men and women who either fail to understand the importance of a communal identity or suppress it out of intellectual vanity. The most obnoxious of the detractors are those who use intimidation to impose their unnatural self-denial on others.

Wæs þa hæl

A Paradox
Years of travelling may bring
surprising results, wholly unforeseen

The Rev<u>d</u> John Lovejoy

Without doubt, I began life with a certain restlessness, for while it is true that I was born in England, of English parents, this was nevertheless at a time and place which were far from auspicious. I began life in East Dulwich, South East London, during the pre-war depression, and the area was heavily bombed, so that it was no doubt a good thing that my parents had decided to move to Sutton, on the Southern outskirts of London, during my first months of life. It was not a good part of Sutton. It was a new street, filled with people from 'The Provinces', who had strange accents, and we were mutual and somewhat distrustful strangers. The street was adjacent to what became a Council tip during the war and my path to school led through a Victorian gas-works, under pipes that leaked smelly chemicals. But that was only after my first school premises was bombed.

Curiously, it was due to the Luftwaffe that I was sent for a while to Cornwall, where I ran rather wild, but had to work on the farm: a farm, be it noted, that had no tractors, but horse-drawn wooden wagons which were in far worse repair than the ones of Constable's famous painting. Cornwall, even at that age, gave me a curious sense of being outside England, but the experience was beneficial. Just after the war, I had another much-needed experience of rural beauty, but this time in the much more English setting of Windsor Great Park, as I stayed with an aunt whose husband worked as a gardener on the Royal Estates. I cannot overestimate the dramatic effect that this interlude had on the consciousness of one who had grown up, except for the period noted above, in the shadow of Sutton gas-works. Among the ancient trees and bracken-bestrewn slopes of the Royal Park, a love of something essentially English was instilled into me, I think. And there, too, I recall that at the tender age of eleven I fell in love.

But something else happened, too, during those early days of childhood, and it was an element of the restlessness which I mentioned at the beginning, a certain looking to distant horizons. In part, of course, this was due to the dreariness of my immediate surroundings, and to the fact that I was rather a bookish only child. But in addition to that, I allowed to grow within me a strong fascination with The North. I found northern friends in the street. At the grammar school which I later attended in Croydon I found a constant friend whose family were from Newcastle upon Tyne. They returned North during my last years at school, and I well remember the journey North along the old A1 on a coach that took twelve hours to arrive! Each pair of passengers had a blanket issued to them to keep off the night chill. I had been joined by a seventeen-year-old young lady who was the last to board the bus, but I can report that her behaviour was impeccable! Anyway, my love of The North was certainly reinforced then, and also later when the same family moved to Cumbria, where I then had a base for exploring the Lake District after finals at the conclusion of student days at King's College London.

The Dean of King's at that time, Sydney Hall Evans, had gathered that I had a love of The North, and so it was that, after a year of post-graduate training in Warminster, I was sent to Newcastle East-End Riverside, to the late-Victorian cobbled streets – all gas-lit when I arrived – of Byker. I was an assistant curate in the Anglican Church, and I began work with genuine culture shock, encountering the full force of the archaic and very musical dialect of that place. There was also an extended family network which seemed to make of the area one huge tribe, and this was the antithesis of what I had grown up with in Sutton.

Much as I loved the riverside area, I also took to exploring the County of Northumberland on my day off. It is a county full of hidden surprises, and much of it has the feeling of being remote and on the very edge of England. Many areas of the County are, indeed, far less accessible to public transport than they were early in the century, when branch railway lines and rural buses extended to most places of consequence. The place-names are steadfastly Anglian, with Bellingham, Eglingham, Whittingham and others all being pronounced with a '-djam' at the end.

After three years I went further North to Choppington, in Bedlingtonshire as some still know it. Ancient family names of Northumbrian sort abounded everywhere, and a few of them astonished me. Visiting one housing area I met a man with un-Northumbrian features and large arched eyebrows. His name was Trevithick. It transpired that his great-great grandfather, a Cornishman, had invented an early form of the steam locomotive. Indeed, in Choppington lies The Wagonway, the site of one of the oldest railway tracks ever. But then, on another housing estate I met individuals with the name Cadwallender – spelt thus. The only likely explanation of this, as I see it in view of the local spelling, is that they are descendants of stragglers from Cadwallader's army, defeated at the Battle of Heavenfield.

So I lived out my love of The North in those days. But this is not an autobiography, and so I must pass over much of personal interest simply by saying that I got married during my time in the North East, but very sadly the marriage broke down, for reasons which I have never entirely been able to fathom.

However, the old restlessness was reawoken by these events, and early in 1970 I decided, in consultation with the Anglican Bishop of Durham, to seek alternative employment overseas for an indeterminate period. I think that I had the notion that, faced with the challenge of rebuilding my life in a new and strange setting, I would be able to reach a new inner equilibrium and deeper personal maturity. Something like that, anyway. In hindsight, I think I can now say that my years of travelling eventually had results which greatly deepened my ties with my land and people of origin rather than the reverse, and now I must explain what I mean. It would seem that the further I got from England, the more I was to discover Englishness. This was the paradox which unfolded itself.

Nigeria – A land of many religions and contrasting identities

Resigning from full-time paid work in the Church, I worked for a while on North Shields Fish-Quay, and then New Malden in South London in a parking-meter factory. There, I met one Sampson Okpodu, a Nigerian, who urged me to consider going to Nigeria, and so I did, as a teacher in the Mid-West State for two years. I had no orientation course, and I was rather vague about where on the map the country was till I arrived there. And the Biafra War had not long finished.

I had two placings during the two years I was there, at a boys' school first, and then, in the second year, a girls' college run by Irish R.C. sisters. I was not teaching English as a subject, but I did note that the students had to read things like Northanger Abbey, which might have occasioned difficulty in some parts of England! The Nigerians have their own somewhat aberrant dialect of English, which they need as there are so many languages within the Federation.

But on me, Nigeria made two sets of very vivid and powerful impressions, first in the local villages of the Ishan Division of the Mid-West State, and then more widely as I began to travel around the Federation during the vacations.

Locally, I came to realise that much survived from what had been essentially a Neolithic culture which had received bronze and iron-age accretions during the most recent millennia. Slavery and smallpox had done their worst, and then there was the most obvious physical result of the colonial period, the replacement of vast areas of primary forest by rubber plantations which, in turn, had been allowed to revert to secondary forest. The area was superabundant in things to eat, and the rainy season never seemed to fail. However, disease was rife and malaria in particular.

The life of the local villages had a very vigorous cultural pattern, according to which 'people' the locals belonged to, each with their own customs, festivals, family structure and distinct language. The Mid-West had a plethora of languages. A person – such as my cook, Andrew – might travel widely, but he would never lose his attachment to his own people, birthplace and village. The agricultural festivals had their own ancient calendar, and seemed to occur in a manner unconnected with the modern calendar and the modern seven-day week. When these festivals occurred, there would be dancing till late around a large wood fire, with a sort of singing in which a haunting and really beautiful melody was repeated for a very long time. I am afraid I have no place for music with Black-American roots, but this music from rural Nigeria drew me powerfully.

Then there were my journeys around the Federation. I will not recount the hair-raising adventures which I had, some of which might have done justice to Indiana Jones, and I reckon that I was lucky to get out alive! But I wanted to observe everything I encountered, and there was much for me to take in. There is an amazing variety of terrain and climate within Nigeria. The ultra-humid and swampy Niger Delta; the somewhat drier and cooler forested zone like the one where my station was situated farther North; the Central Plateau with its poor soils and harsh rocky contours; the vast semi-desert areas of the North. Then there was a little known highland area in the far East of Nigeria which had been the northern section of the German Cameroon in colonial times. Here, I found the Mambilla Plateau, where there was clean, fresh water from mountain streams and a forestry of a more temperate climate, managed at that time by Canadian expatriates. Here, I crossed a crocodile-infested river using liana vine.

The human variety, culturally and even racially, matched the range of terrain. Yoruba in the South West, Igbo in the South-East, along with the many peoples and languages of the Mid-West and the Delta area, such as Esan and Ijaw. In the North, there were the Hausa, who were largely cattlemen, wiry in build and fiery in temperament. The Plateau, to which Jos was the gateway, was the home of very archaic human cultures. The remoter areas of the North-East, around Maiduguri, had different people again, towards the shores of Lake Chad. Religions, too, were diverse, with Islam dominant in the North, and different rites of Christianity in the South, but indigenous religions were also very much alive, and syncretistic cults could also be found. I could not always tell whether some of the strange ceremonies that I stumbled across on occasion were religious in character, or whether they were simply cultural celebrations or re-enactments. The distinction is bound to be blurred.

What did I learn from all this rich and contrasting human diversity? I think that even then I came to understand that the diversity was highly necessary from a human point of view: that is, that the plurality of human cultures, each with its own integrity and aspects of excellence, was something which ought not to be lost, however much a veneer of modernity might supervene. I began to see that the human richness in all its various modes, themselves required in part by the diversities of terrain and climate, was something which was necessarily received from a remoter past, and that human cultures, while they may be transmuted from time to time, must never be diminished or changed in such a way as to alienate them from themselves.

What I did not realise then at all clearly, although the penny was to drop later, is that the lessons which I was confronted with at that time so urgently and vividly also applied elsewhere, and not least to England and to my own people, the English! Let us consider. England is so called because the main southern part of Britain was invaded and settled in the early fifth century – if not before that in some cases – by groups of closely related Germanic peoples whose principal appellation was *Englisc*. But the land which they took control of was, and is, a land of amazing contrasts. As you proceed from the South East to the North West you encounter about every sort of geological stratum imaginable, and when the English arrived there were vast areas of forest and fen, with drainage systems that have since undergone extensive modification. Furthermore, there are surprising contrasts of climate in England for such a relatively small territory. England rests on a transition zone between continental and Atlantic weather systems, and our northerly latitude, while mild because of the Gulf Stream, nevertheless leads to a very significant temperature gradation from south to north, and also with changes of altitude, so that people have to exercise caution in moorland and upland areas.

But it is not just the land which offers these contrasts. I have already remarked the regional distinctions of dialect and custom which I encountered while very young, first because of the drift to the Capital during the 'thirties, and then when I transferred my attentions to the North, though not without some contact with the West during National Service and in my post-graduate year. Of course, the human diversity – at any rate among the English themselves – was never anywhere near as great as in Nigeria, for the simple reason that the English have always been essentially one people even though not at first politically united in one kingdom. I can say, however, that English diversity, up to the time of my youth, was something which was perceived as being remarkable, even without considering the Celtic areas beyond.

There is a sense in which England is a bit like Dr. Who's *tardis*, in that what looks like a small land on the global atlas nevertheless seems to contain long distances and a number of areas that feel remote, and not easy to reach. Our time-scale, too, is impressive. Over a third of our recorded history in this land lies before the cataclysmic, but not definitive, Norman Conquest. And we know that we have a continental pre-history before that. The Old English language itself contains some enigmatic clues. Our word 'butter', for instance, which Old English seems to have inherited from Primitive Germanic, indicating a contact with the Greeks at a very early date, and the languages are cognate in any case, though distantly.

Italy – A country and people with cultural continuity and cultural awareness

I chose not to return to Nigeria, mainly because school-teaching is not my natural mode of life, and after some casting around for a sense of direction in England, and spending time on international work camps, I travelled by train to Milan, and found work in a language school, teaching English.

Milan impressed me heavily in a variety of ways. There was the wealth of impressive architecture in the Centre, and the array of cultural activities and art forms proper to an Italian city. The trams drew my attention, too, and I found that I could stand dreamily on the rear platform, watching a leafy avenue recede from me as I stared from this smoothly moving rail-car, which made but a pleasant, if plaintive, wailing sound, punctuated by a clanging bell. There were, too, the *piazze*, for whereas in modern England you find a traffic junction, period, in Milan as elsewhere on the Continent the junction revolves round an impressive edifice commemorating some momentous event in the nation's history, and on the periphery you will find more than one *bar-cafe* where people of like mind can meet and exchange thoughts on all topics of interest to them.

The cumulative effect on my mind, at that time, was a shaking-up of my imagination of something like seven on the mental Richter Scale. I began to realise consciously what I had been learning unwittingly in Nigeria. I started to make a personal critique of the Modern Civilisation (to use a deliberately vague term). I discovered the Green Movement for myself, as I had not then realised that it had already come into being, and I became aware of a number of things in the Modern Civilisation which I could now see were increasingly dangerous.

In fact, I began to ask the question "What do we mean by a human 'culture', or 'civilisation'"? On these themes I started to write reams of stuff to my friends in England.

At that time, of course, I had little opportunity of applying what I was learning to the situation in England itself, although one thing helped, and that was my paid job in TEFL, which led me to examine the character and structure of the modern English language in its received standard British-English form. I was fascinated by it, and increasingly impressed. The English Principal of the language school, before he retired, reminded me that Modern English was demonstrably descended from the Old English language, 'Anglo-Saxon' as we both then called it, and thus was sown the seed of a later increasing interest in the Old form – *englisc*.

While in Milan, I came to believe that in England there was a relatively high cultural impoverishment, this being due, I thought, to a number of related factors, such as strong class divisions, the early arrival of the Industrial Revolution in its earliest and crudest form, the element of utilitarianism in nineteenth-century philosophical thinking, the concentration of effort into expanding and maintaining the Empire, and the effect of two World Wars. Moreover, the high degree of fragmentation of the prevailing religion meant, I saw, that the modern English lacked an advantage which Greece, Poland, and even Norway, seem to have had, when it comes to encouragement of cultural continuity and integrity – not to mention Italy.

Algiers – A city with deep scars and communal fault-lines

After two years I left Italy, and after a visit to the U.K. made my way to Milan only to leave immediately for Marseilles, whence I took a crossing by sea to Algiers. I arrived at the seaport only to find the place utterly deserted, so I simply walked into the Country, though one man did appear after a bit to stamp my passport. I had arrived on the first Friday which was being observed officially and nationally as the day of rest in that country!

I did find the Language School, and two Irish members of staff were waiting for me to accompany me to my apartment. I have to say that I had rather an uncomfortable time in Algiers, and after a while I began to see why. The war of independence which ended with the Treaty of Evian was not as simple as it seems. Besides the independence issue was the tension between mainland France and the *pied-noirs*; and between Arab and Berber. The Berbers refused, in many instances, even to learn the Arabic alphabet. Unable to use their own language publicly, they used French. Another alarming trend was the population explosion in this previously very French city. There was also a growing tension, even then, between those who practised a rather nominal form of Islam, and those who wanted something dogmatic and thoroughgoing.

I am not sure what all this was teaching me in a more general way, but two separate incidents are worthy of note.

One day, I was rummaging round in the rear of a newly reopened shop near the Casbah. It was a Bible Shop, and Government permission had been granted. To my astonishment, in the dust and gloom of an old cupboard, I found some old printing plates bearing a script which I had never before seen. It dawned on me that they were in the old Berber script and language, which were both politically suppressed at that time. We had them spirited away – I am not sure where! Looking at the script at the time, I thought it was not far removed from the ancestral Phoenician script which, I think, underlies a number of modern alphabets. Perhaps, here, is an impulse to the study of indigenous scripts in general, and to *futhorc*[1] which we are rediscovering slowly, in the case of *Englisc*.

The other event concerned a visit I made to the British Council library in Algiers. I was looking for language material, as I was still teaching in my first year in the city. My eye alighted on a copy of *Teach Yourself Old English*, by Leslie Blakeley. I have to confess – and I was forty-two at the time – that I really had not been aware before that, that the old language was currently accessible for study! Nobody at school, at any level, had ever referred to the Old English language, though there was once a rather half-hearted attempt I recall to introduce us to the Middle-English of Chaucer.

Apart from making me want to begin learning Old English, it also made me ask myself why there was such a low level of awareness, among modern English people, of the existence and present available status of O.E. as a classical language. It could well be that to increase the level of awareness of the Old English language will be a principal way of raising awareness of the Old English period and its culture generally. I rather

---

[1] The *futhorc* is an English version of the runic alphabet, and is so named after the first six runic letters in the sequence; just as *alphabet* is constructed from the first two letters, *alpha* and *beta*, in the Greek sequence of letters.

think so, for this can operate even where there is no desire to learn the language. Even to see Old English written down, whether in *futhork*, Insular Script, or an editor's preferred convention for the use of the modern alphabet, is a powerful reminder of the people and the times when the language was in daily use.

Well, I did discover Old English for myself in the end. But in Algiers?

The Kimberley Plateau, North West Australia
A Dreamtime Fastness

I remained no longer in Algiers than in Milan, but the impetus to my imagination continued, and I developed a desire to have contact with an archaic tribal people. I returned to the U.K. long enough to research possibilities, and eventually found a post in the far North West of Australia which involved commuting between the township of Wyndham on the Cambridge Gulf and Oombulgurri, which was an Aboriginal station on the Forrest River.

I did not succeed in doing very much either to or for the Aborigines, and this was no doubt a good thing, for these unfortunate people had had more than enough of people doing things to or for them. I wanted to learn from them, and had to be prepared for them to make things known to me in their own time and in their own way. I had been hoping to help them to recover the local language, and reduce it to a written form, but unfortunately I was, I estimate, some ten years too late for that. This should remind us how fortunate we are, in England, to have written records in the Old English language, for *Englisc* has had to reach us through centuries of indifference and neglect. The same could be said of the Celtic languages, I suppose, including in their case the modern form as well.

It will be asked what sort of things I learnt from the Aborigines, and in what ways they reinforced what I already knew. I will list the main things now.

1. A land where Mesolithic cultures
survived intact till very recently.

The Aborigines, generally, were what we might call Middle Stone Age peoples. We may also use the term 'archaic tribal people'. But these are our terms, not theirs, and there are faults in our perspective, for the nineteenth century concept of 'Progress' has bitten very deep into our thinking and conceptual system. Aboriginal societies in Australia were just as complete, as valid human cultures, as our own, and in many ways, perhaps, even more so. It is just that they travelled light through this world, and such technology as they had was for the most part within their heads. They exercised the cultural choice of fitting in with the environment, rather than harnessing it, exploiting it, taming it.

This is important for us because it is probable that the whole human race passed through a Mesolithic phase over a very long time period, and that the Aborigines of Australia were unusual only because they persisted longer in that phase. I do not think that the peoples who spoke the Primitive Germanic language could have been far removed from Mesolithic culture, because words which the Neolithic peoples would have found useful seem often to be other than Indo-European. Be that as it may, Mesolithic cultures in general show us a lot about the central stuff of raw humanity in an archaic presentation.

These archaic Mesolithic peoples tend to concentrate on the things that really matter, and I list:–

- The 'Dreamtime' and the Ancient 'Law', in which a system of mythology will have been handed down from remote antiquity, in such a way as to underpin a current religious system and a communal code of behaviour, governing all areas of communal life.

- The relationship with the territory, whereby the particular people in question inherits a system of communal survival within the territory to which they belong and to which they have always belonged.

- The Relationship System, whereby human relationships of various degrees are regulated according to the requirements of the archaic Law – albeit with some flexibility – so as to form a communal pattern of interwoven types and degrees of relationship, modulated by differences of sex and age. The relationship system serves as the political system in these archaic societies.

- The Initiation Ceremonies. Social Anthropologists delight in studying the *rites of passage*, and I will not dwell on this point in detail because my experience was with a culture which was extremely fractured anyway. But I will make the point that the near-universal occurrence of these things in archaic societies suggests that any society which omits them in any form does so at its communal peril, and is not a complete human society.

- The Language. I have already mentioned my relative failure in trying to recover one such, but there was another difficulty which I only realised towards the end of my time among the people of Oombulgurri. I asked one older man why it was so hard to recover the old language, and he replied only with hesitance, at first simply scratching strange patterns on the sand at our feet. The gist of his reply, though, which I did elicit this time, was that the old language was regarded as part and parcel with the Ancient Law, and the terms of the Ancient Law were very largely broken now. The Aborigines were no longer able to live according to the Ancient Law in its entirety, and so the use of the old language would have been too uncomfortable a reminder of this fact.

Such were the main elements of the archaic cultures, the details of which were filled in culture by culture. A realisation of these things in Old English studies will help to give us a better perspective. Instead of comparing Anglo-Saxon society with what we have now (whatever that really is), we can ask instead how Old English society differed from the archaic tribal societies from which we are all descended anyway. Further, in that the archaic societies supply us with a list of the really basic and fundamental questions of human existence, we can then ask how the Old English people managed to address the same fundamental human issues in practice.

2. The importance of the persistence of human cultures over long periods of time.

The Mesolithic cultures of Australia present us with cultural continuity and persistence in what, to our modern perspective, seems an extreme form. We may believe that change did occur, but that this probably happened in cycles, reversibly, according to fluctuations of the Earth's climatic systems and orbital variations. There is no answer to the question 'When was the Dreamtime?', for archaic societies did not have the sense of history unfolding in an ever-extending chronology or events. Perhaps the ancient myths do present us with symbolic representations of cataclysmic events in a very remote past, but we have no means of unlocking such symbolism. Rather, we have to see the 'Dreamtime' as being effectively outside time, and the myths have to be viewed in terms of their present functions.

This said, we can assume that the aboriginal societies have persisted for many tens of thousands of years, without dramatic changes, and since this must have been the case elsewhere in the world once upon a time, we may be led to think that human beings need cultural continuity, and that rapid and accelerating change may be extremely bad for us in ways that we do not realise.

In Old English times, there were relatively stable periods, and there were other times when change and instability were forced on them from outside, either by invasion, or by famine and pestilence. The Seventh Century conversion was a change, but the impact on the shape and form of Old English society may be less than a lot of people suppose. It seems to me likely that the Christian Faith, in the form that it took then, for the most part filled the gaps which the retreat of the Old Religion had left. But we live in a part of the world which seems prone to change, and so we have to be quite specific as to the period we mean when we are talking about the characteristics of Old English society. But that said, the people who lived in the Old English times would not have experienced change in the relentless, ongoing and accelerating way that it has taken in our own times. Rather, there would have been cataclysmic events from time to time, followed by periods of slow return to a normality which would be in certain respects different from the previous *status quo*.

3. The importance of plurality and diversity for human societies.

Australia is an island continent, and is about the same size as the U.S.A. if we leave Alaska out of account. There was no 'Aboriginal Society', anymore than there is a 'European Society', for the land as a whole comprises many climates and types of terrain, so that the Mesolithic societies, which by definition mould themselves to the particular terrain in which they live, differ from one another quite remarkably. Although I worked in the Kimberley, I was able to meet, from time to time, some of the Desert Aborigines, for they were often picked up after drunken brawls, and left to sober up in Wyndham Jail, which was effectively a drying-out centre. Indeed, it is the only jail I know where the perimeter fence was intended to keep people out rather than in. The Desert Aborigines were racially markedly different from the peoples of the Kimberley Plateau.

Now there is strong evidence that Australia, in recent prehistoric times has had progressive changes of climate. That is why, as my own father remarked during a visit to South West Australia in 1982, the trees seem to be struggling to survive. Australian trees often do better in another country.

Meanwhile, human societies have also had to adapt to the changes of the last tens of thousands of years, and a plurality of human cultures offered the best chance of survival for the human population as a whole.

When we consider the case of Old English society, it can hardly be a matter of regret that the political unification of England took so long to bring about. Old English society must have been all the more vigorous because of the juxtaposition of the different kingdoms. On the other hand, it might also be argued that the Old English kingdoms would have done well to have learned earlier how to co-operate against a common external foe, as was the case with the Hellenic societies of Ancient Greece. Classical Greece, one supposes, was always united in some degree by the Aegean Sea, rather than by land, and perhaps the English needed to have maintained longer their recognised early prowess in ship construction and seamanship.

4. An Aboriginal nightmare – the loss of their womenfolk.

When I arrived in Oombulgurri, I suppose that even I was hoping for things to happen. They didn't. Only, every time the Unemployment Benefit cheques arrived in Wyndham, the Aboriginal men went by charter plane to Wyndham and went in for bouts of heavy drinking, after first getting rid of the cash at the Liquor Store.

For a long time I tried to puzzle out why this self-destructiveness was so pervasive amongst the whole male population of a certain age-group, and among a lesser number of the women. The usual explanation was that the ancient culture had been smashed by the arrival of the cattle industry in the North, and the archaic tribal Law was no longer operative in its entirety. This is no doubt true in some measure, but human societies can recover from a great deal of disruption, and I think that the Old English culture could be cited as an example.

It was when I returned to modern England that the main explanation became clear to me. The cattlemen, earlier in the century, had not only shot up the Aborigines on occasion, when they hunted across the European men's boundaries, but they did something worse. They did employ the Aborigines as stockmen, but there was a terrible price to pay, for the women began to yearn for the things which the Europeans had, and the Europeans used the Aboriginal women for sexual relief. No further explanation is needed for pervasive alcoholic destructiveness which I saw. The men had been losing their own womenfolk, and life became a nightmare from which they saw alcohol (in the form of cheap port) as the only escape. I hope that the human race as a whole has learned better by now, but I doubt it.

5. The beginnings of cultural reconstruction.

The last section was rather a sombre one, but I was with the Aboriginal community at a difficult time. When I visited them later during a Christmas vacation after I returned to Australia to work in Perth, I saw many signs of hope. A new generation was now growing up which wanted some thing different from the alcoholic despair of their fathers and uncles. Western Australia began to take a live interest in the Community Special School, and sent a supply of teachers who were sympathetic to Aboriginal culture, and knew what they were doing. And then, there were the children themselves. In many ways they took their own education in hand. When I arrived on the visit, the children took me to a waterfall as the rainy season was beginning, and got me to jump off cliffs into the rock-pool below. These children also have a good sense of humour!

Of course, they cannot go back to the hunter-gatherer existence that their forebears had had, but they can be aware of it; they can be proud of it; and also they can undertake the task of choosing which elements of the old way of life can be combined with elements from the new, in a viable way for the present time. In all this, as a constant background, is the fact that the modern Aboriginal settlement of Oombulgurri lies within the same territory which they always inhabited, and the terrain as a whole, in that wild, remote area, remains largely what it always was, awe-inspiring, humbling to the human spirit, and a challenge to human powers of survival.

Can those with Old English interests find inspiration here? I like to think so. I do believe, along with many, that we are faced in our own day with an immense task of cultural reconstruction, though we can no more go back to the way of life of Old English times than the Aborigines can revert to their ways of before the European settlement.

If I am right, then our task is not entirely dissimilar to that of the Aborigines, in that modern English people, those that is who are culturally aware, need to make themselves familiar with what is known about the Old English times, so that they have the right sort of inspiration for the present activities, drawn from the right sources. Not to do this would be to allow, if only by default, some other source of cultural inspiration to shape and mould our current endeavours of cultural reconstruction. And this is where I see the importance, in large measure, of the studies and activities which Ða Engliscan Gesiðas (The English Companions) engage in, for although their studies are strictly to do with discovery of what is the truth about the Old English period, nevertheless it is modern English people, for the most part, who will be found taking a lively interest in the Anglo-Saxons, their language and culture. People of other ethnic backgrounds would be entirely welcome in Ða Engliscan Gesiðas, I am certain, but I do not see them, and the reason is surely that they are drawn to other sources of inspiration as the founts of their respective cultures.

As a modern Englishman myself, I have believed, since returning to England in recent years, that a movement towards cultural reconstruction among our own ethnic community is both highly desirable and very urgent.

Huntly, West Aberdeenshire
A year in the North-East of Scotland

As this is not an autobiography, I do not have to explain the steps that led me from North West Australia, one of the Earth's hottest places, to the North-East of Scotland, just when a quite severe winter was approaching. Somewhere between, I was on an archaeological dig near an Anglo-Saxon cemetery, but that is another story. The dig was to have momentous consequences for me later.

But in Strathbogie, as the area around Huntly is known, I was simply impressed by the sheer Scottishness of everything around me: the salmon rivers, the foothills of the North Grampian, the ruined castles, the distilleries, the forests, the granitic architecture, the low clouds. In the smaller villages towards the Grampians the old Doric dialect could be heard; arguably the most archaic surviving form of English, though I should like to know what others think.

I was working for a year as a gardener at the Alexander Scott Memorial Hospital, and was staying in the attic of a massive granite town building in the centre of Huntly, only two doors away from where the well-known writer George MacDonald had once lived. In those days I did watch TV in the evening, to relax.

While viewing in this way one evening in June 1986, I happened to watch an instalment of the series *The Blood of the British* on Channel Four, presented by the archaeologist Catherine Hills. I was horrified to find the view being set forth that the basic identity of the population in Britain remained essentially unchanged, despite some disturbance from some bands of marauders from time to time, the Angles and Saxons being named among them somewhere within a list of relatively unimportant chance newcomers.

This distortion of the facts incensed me so much that I immediately wrote to complain to the Independent Broadcasting Authority, and then set about preparing a large paper on the subject of cultural disintegration and degradation among the modern English People. This paper I then addressed to the then Home Secretary, The Right Hon. Sir Douglas Hurd. And in reply:–

> Thank you for you letter of 29 May to the Home Secretary enclosing your very interesting analysis of a problem facing society today.
>
> Your paper will be studied with care.

I was a little bit worried about the last lines. Was it just me, or was I really being watched for a while after that?

Anyway, there are probably many ways whereby those in power might try to obliterate a nation or ethnic group, but Catherine Hills' method was rather subtle. Using the Broadcast Media, you <u>define</u> a nation out of existence. They never really existed in the first place!

All of which demonstrates a principle which I have in the past discussed with other members (gesiðas) of Ða Engliscan Gesiðas. In that Fellowship, which is strictly non-sectarian and non-political, we strictly avoid involvement in any matters of contention concerning the English People at the present time. But when it comes to attempts to falsify the events of the Old English period, or to inflict damage on the sites dating from those days, then we feel free to raise a voice in protest. That, after all, was how Ða Engliscan Gesiðas started.

After a year, I left Scotland for a while to return to Australia, this time near Perth W.A., as I needed to be able to send more money to my two teenage children, and in Western Australia I was able to do so when they needed it.

Perth, Western Australia
Evidence of transferred Englishness

Suddenly arriving on my Aussie cousin's doorstep I found work as quickly as I could, and took employment in an engineering works where we applied rubber linings to steel mining machinery. The work was heavy, noisy, dirty, and dangerous, and I loved it! As I was used largely to assemble the iron-ore screen decks for the Pilbara iron-ore extraction companies, I had rather a central place, I felt, in the Western Australian economy.

All of which might seem irrelevant but for one thing. The works radio, which in any case was usually inaudible because of the much preferable noise of the machinery, was situated inside, whereas I was in the yard at the back, and was free to listen to Radio 6NR, the like of which does not seem to exist in England. Radio 6NR specialised in archaic recordings and music from very early in the 20th century, if not at times from the end of the last one. Thus, truck drivers who rounded the corner into the yard would suddenly hear, *I heard a brown bird singing…*; or *Less than the dust beneath thy chariot wheel…*; or *Come, come, come to me Thora…*; and many other such items from the days of aspidistras, macassar oil, and the Constitutional, as well as The Raj and British naval supremacy. The recordings, of course, were either scratchy 78's if they had not been remastered, or even, in some cases, shellac cylinders.

I had not realised, till then, how averse I had become to Transatlantic Pop in all of its ramifications, and I saw that we have to go back rather a long way to find a time when we were not being overwhelmed by one popular musical form or another from the U.S.A. Not that even what I was hearing on Radio 6NR was without its distortions, from the point of view of someone wanting a truly English popular cultural form. The British Imperial backdrop itself distorted popular musical development, as witness the popularity of Amy Woodforde Finden's *Indian Love Lyrics* and others by Albert Ketelby. Still, I wish I could listen now to Radio 6 NR, because I really cannot accept Transatlantic Pop any more: it seems so alien to me, and even downright horrible. I get some relief by listening to LGR (no, not GLR) – London Greek Radio. At least the Greeks remain refreshingly Greek.

Perhaps it was this musical experience which inspired me later, while in Perth W.A., to write a leaflet expounding the beginnings and origins of English society and culture, as I wanted a convenient hand-out to use later while on a Long Distance Run which I hoped to do when I arrived back in England. For I had to return in order to begin caring for my increasingly elderly parents by this time, in 1988.

England as I found it on my return to my land of origin, in 1988

Thus, at last I returned to England at the end of the eighties after restless wanderings over many years, after I had found it necessary to leave the North-East, in 1970. I returned with the leaflets which I have mentioned, and with the firm intention of going on Long Distance Runs around England, in the hope of meeting people and awakening an interest in the Old English basis of our identity.

I have to say that at the time when I returned to England, I did not like what I saw. Indeed, I was so disturbed by what I saw around me, or saw and heard on the Broadcast Media, that I started to write papers rather in the vein of the earlier ones that I had written while in Scotland, in Huntly.

Here, I can do no more than to indicate my main areas of disquiet in a series of headings, each of which could have been expanded into the size of a chapter or even a whole book. For this purpose, I continued to use the word *deculturalisation*, a rather appropriately ugly word which I had used in my paper to the Home Secretary, in 1986.

The headings which I would use to indicate my main departures of thought at that time were these:–

- Dismay at the extent of deculturalisation in Greater London, among young English people.

- The massive degree of Americanisation of popular culture.

- The disregard of, or positive attacks on, English culture and origins, on the part of Broadcast Media.

- The evident decay of the Modern English language under the impact of social and economic change, and under foreign influence.

- A near universal amnesia in respect of the Old English period and its culture, among ordinary people.

- The prevalence of double standards, whereby other nations and ethnic communities were often being encouraged in an awareness of identity and cultural expression which was being condemned or denied in the case of the English.

- A refusal to listen to complaints from English people on the part of official agencies and departments, and a lack of any representative voice for English people – this in strong contrast with the clearly evident means of common expression which other ethnic communities had.

In 1989, with this kind of thinking in my mind, I did indeed set off on a series of Long Distance Runs, working my way slowly through England, doing about twenty-five miles per day, and staying overnight in Bed-and-Breakfast accommodation. I found that I could make some of my most valuable contacts with ordinary people when I stopped for lunch, or at breakfast in the B&B place. For the most part, however, I was alone with my own thoughts while running, and the physical effect of running sharpened my imagination and perception so that I was able to appreciate the English scenery and the successive regional characteristics as I passed through them. I was not always able to avoid main roads, but where possible I used a network of minor roads as indicated on a good map and also took local advice about off-route pathways and tracks. National networks are beginning to appear, such as those under the heading of *sustrans*.

I had to stop these activities for a long time because of caring duties at home, but in the meantime I had been receiving a booklist produced by one of the jurisdictions of the Orthodox Church operating in England. Because of the interest that they have in the history of Christianity in England before the Great Schism of 1054, the Orthodox Church included in its booklists some titles produced by Anglo-Saxon Books, and when I actually acquired one of these titles the book contained an advertisement for Ða Engliscan Gesiðas, which I was then able to join.

My discovery of like-minded people in this way was timely, because previously, in my isolation, I had been making some plans to launch an organisation of some sort to promote interest in the beginnings and origins of English culture and national identity, but now it seemed that this was already happening, so I was saved the trouble!

I have mentioned the tangential part that the Orthodox Church played in my discovery of Ða Engliscan Gesiðas through the common interest in the Old English period, and it is not my purpose to discuss matters such as ecclesiastical allegiances, but in fact I did become attached to the Greek Orthodox Church as it operates in this country, and this meant that recently I have had to cope with the Greek language and also make friends with the Greek Community. I have to say that in a place like London the Greek Community sets a very encouraging example in their persistence and determination to maintain their culture and identity, which they value and enjoy tremendously, while living in a setting which, as we know, is becoming increasingly hostile to any such purpose, whether one is Greek or English. I hope it will be understood, then, if I mention my new-found friends.

At one function which I attended when I first contacted the Greeks, I was seated at a table in an upper room of the church building, and on the wall appeared, not holy pictures, but fierce-looking nineteenth-century warriors! The Greeks do have an advantage in that they are able to appeal to recent struggles to survive as a nation, whereas more recent English history has been submerged, rather, in the British Imperial phase of our history. As regards the classical phase of their history, I think that the Greeks have a problem reverse to that of our own, for Classical Greek culture is so famous that it tends to overshadow the present, whereas we are struggling to win recognition for the Old English culture.

I can report that Andreas, my table-companion that evening, recalled the part that Lord Byron played in the history of independence of his people.

In any case, the Greeks have a tremendous advantage in that they have a very distinct language and alphabet, and also have a common religion (as have certain other nations) which serves to cement their culture and social structure. But a lot of the young members of the Greek community no longer speak Greek, and this is becoming a problem. And it is our problem too. What I often hear in the street or on the radio is not what I would recognise as English. While we, in groups such as Ða Engliscan Gesiðas, rightly turn our attention to Old English, I think that it is also right that we should resist the degradation and impoverishment of the modern language in its British form. Other nations and peoples may use English, but surely the English themselves have the right – even a duty – to value and develop their own standard form of the language which took shape among us in the first instance. One's language is a very intimate and integral part of one's humanity.

In all, I am hoping that my attachment to the Greek Community will help me to have a sharper perspective of the problems faced by the English Community as we face the task, as I see it, of cultural reconstruction and reaffirmation of what is ours.

In conclusion – English culture and identity perceived in many other settings

I began by mentioning the paradox that the further I got from England, the more I was to discover Englishness. Perhaps I should summarize very briefly what I learnt.

In the North-East of England, I was confronted with a lower working-class English society which, at that time, had not undergone the disintegration and fragmentation which I had grown up with in Greater London. This gave me a sense of grief for something lost. I also saw a late form of a strong regional culture.

In Nigeria, especially as I travelled round by pick-up vehicle or motorbike, I came to see the rich diversity of the many regions of that large African country, and my sense that such diversity is fundamentally necessary to humanity was starting to take shape.

In Italy, surrounded by beautiful cultural forms and architecture, as well as by the vivid and expressive language, I began to see the immense importance of cultural integrity, and began to realise that human beings cannot exist without a culture or civilisation to grow up in. I also started to question what the Modern Civilisation was, and what was wrong with it.

In Algiers, besides seeing and sensing the tensions which remained after the recent turmoil surrounding independence, I rediscovered the Old English language in an unlikely place, and – through seeing the contrast between Arabic and Berber – I saw the vital connection between language and culture in that setting.

While with the Aboriginal Community of Oombulgurri, Forest River, N.W. Australia, I learned to be patient and in that way learned so much.

- I saw, in all its starkness and horror, the effects of cultural devastation and collapse.

- At the same time, much remained under the surface, and I saw the amazing persistence of cultural elements which had been transmitted, one supposes, through many thousands of years.

- There was still an awareness of The Dreamtime, the core and source, mythically expressed, of the people and their culture and of the land to which they belonged, as well as of all the living things on it.

- There was the prominence, as in Mesolithic cultures generally, of those elements of human culture which are vitally important, and which must be successfully addressed in any viable human way of life.

- There was the sad loss of the indigenous language, in that particular instance, along with the development of their own very distinctive Aboriginal dialect of English, retaining much of the phonetic system and many words from the old language.

- Lastly, there was the growing self-confidence of a new generation, with a determination to undertake a cultural reconstruction, using what they could from the past, with such elements of the modern way of life as they would need in order that they might now relate to the world as they found it.

Since all human beings are descended from archaic human societies, it behoves us to learn as much as we can from them and from what has happened to them in the wake of contact with late European societies.

In Scotland, I suppose, I learned to speak up when I began to realise that English culture and identity were being misrepresented. It also occurred to me that the English can only gain from the Scots' own attempts to express their self-awareness and national identity.

And finally, I have been presented with the example of the Greeks, whose own communal determination to express their culture and identity is evident within England itself, and not least within those urban parts of England where the English themselves have suffered most from disintegration of their way of life.

As a result of what I have been able to observe, in all these settings and in many and various ways, I wish now to encourage my own people, the English People, to take heart from what happens elsewhere, but also to lose any complacency which they might have had. Our task is to recover an understanding of what a human society and a human culture truly mean, and then to begin to reconstruct our own English way of life, using whatever we can recover from the Old English period for sources and inspiration, and whatever lessons we may learn from what has happened to other peoples elsewhere, for I believe that the necessary plurality of human cultures is an axiom which we may safely use, and. surely the English culture has its place within that rich patchwork quilt of human ways of life which the human spirit, at its best, has always welcomed and accepted.

Let us recall, too, that cultural reconstruction is not an unprecedented exercise. I would ask my compatriots to read afresh the words of Alfred, King of the West Saxons, as he writes on the state of learning in England in a letter prefixed to his version of Gregory the Great's *Pastoral Care*.

ða ic ða ðis eall gemunde ða gemunde ic eac hu ic geseah, ærðæmðe hit eall forhergod wære ך forbærned, hu ða ciricean giond eall Angelcynn stodon maðma ך boca gefyldæ ond eac micel menigeo Godes ðiowa ך ða swiðe lytle fiorme ðara boca wiston, forðæmðe hie hiora nan wuht ongiotan ne meahton ond þæt wæs forðæmðe hie næron on hiora agen geðiode awritene. Swelce hie cwæden:

Ure ieldran, ða ðe ðas stowa ær hioldon, hie lufodon wisdom ך ðurh ðone hie begeaton welan ך us læfdon. Her mon mæg giet gesion hiora swæð, ac we him ne cunnon æfterspyrigean, ך forðæm we habbað nu ægðer forlæten ge ðone welan ge ðone wisdom, forðæmðe we noldon to ðæm spore mid ure mode onlutan.

When I reflected on all this, I then recalled how I saw – before it was all plundered and burnt down – how the churches throughout all England stood filled with treasures and books and a great throng of God's servants; and they knew very little benefit from those books, because they could not understand anything in them, for they were not written in their own language. Thus they spoke:

"Our forefathers, who previously held these places, they loved wisdom and through it they came by wealth and left it to us. One can still see their track here, but we cannot follow them for we have now given up both that wealth and that wisdom, because we did not wish to hold to the track with our hearts."

Translation by Stephen Pollington

This chapter has taken the form of a sort of odyssey, I suppose, but this is enough of my travellers' tales and reminiscences from far away and sometimes not so far away.

Perhaps I have had to omit a lot (the good bits?), but then I have not intended to give a continuous connected discourse. Instead, I hope that many of my recollections are relevant, and help to cast light on the English situation from various perspectives.

Currently, at the time of writing, I have to remain where I am as I may be needed in special ways by those who are very close to me, but it is my hope that again, in the not distant future, I may go on Long Distance Runs across England in order to help raise awareness of the Old English basis of our culture and identity as a people and nation.

Along with whatever I may do in that way, it is also my earnest hope that all who hold England dear, and wish to affirm the continued existence of the people who call themselves English, may likewise find ways of rekindling the ardent interest in the beginnings and origins of our people, together with its current expression, which is surely required of us in these days as it was in the days of Alfred Athelwulfing.

Our Englishness

Geoffrey Littlejohns

The contempt of intellectuals for England and Englishness is not a recent phenomenon. Nearly sixty years ago George Orwell gave this description in his essay *The Lion and the Unicorn*.

> England is perhaps the only great country whose intellectuals are ashamed of their own nationality. In left-wing circles it is always felt that there is something slightly disgraceful in being an Englishman and that it is a duty to snigger at every English institution from horseracing to suet puddings.'[1]

Orwell hoped that this phenomenon would not last. He considered that, faced with the menace of foreign invasion in 1940, the intellectual mood would change and 'patriotism and intelligence will [have] come together again'. But of course it did not happen. The sneering and sniggering at nationhood not only persisted but it grew in the decades that followed his death to reach far beyond those whom Orwell identified as 'left-wing intellectual'. By the sixties many young people, affected by the fashion for cynical and hedonistic behaviour, had absorbed this anti-patriotic attitude. By the seventies the attitude had become entrenched. Contempt for our country was then so strong that for many politicians and civil servants the remaining objective of the British state could only be the smooth management of its decline. In the eighties and nineties the process seemed complete. Intellectuals of the self-styled 'post-modernist' breed sprang up who eagerly pronounced the death of nationhood. They were declaring that the era of the nation-state was over.

There is no reason why the rest of us should accept without question this assertion from the introverted intellectual elite. We should examine carefully the confident proclamation that the death of nationhood is at hand. It may well be true that the established state system is under pressure and changing. It is certainly true that in the decades since the Second World War supra-national bodies have vastly enlarged their powers. Not just the European Union and the European Court of Justice, but the World Trade Organisation, the IMF and the World Bank have been handed the authority to impose their will and undermine the sovereignty of established states. These supranational bodies are not only meddling with commercial, financial and fiscal affairs, but intrude into areas of social policy. The flow of political policy-making, moreover, seems to be strongly in their favour. Politicians and civil servants, rather than defending the powers and prerogatives of the states they are employed to administer, are eager to participate in arrangements and agreements, vague and obscure to the general public, which further the march towards globalism. The British state, for instance, has connived by its passivity in the ruin of thousands of British fishermen

---

[1] George Orwell, *The Collected Essays, Journalism and Letters Volume 2*, Penguin 1968.

and farmers by accepting the schemes of the European Union to advance the interests of others. The British state is no longer willing to serve its original and prime purpose – to defend the interests of the peoples of Britain against the deceit of outsiders. What we have regarded as nation-states are rapidly weakening but does that mean that the advance of globalism is unstoppable? Should we believe and accept that our future world is to be one in which a universal cosmopolitan state will rule and we, as subjects, will slither down into a condition of a passive, homogenised and undifferentiated populace. In this world of dying nation-states, must the nation die too? Before we believe in and accept that death, we must first consider the view that the established and declining state system is indeed a system of real nation-states.

What is a nation-state? To answer this we must first ask what a nation is and how it is created. One interpretation declares that a nation is created as an after-effect of the earlier formation of a state. This certainly applies in the French Republic. If we consider the state and nation there it is clear that citizenship acknowledged by the French Republic acts as the definition of what French nationality is. The individual achieves his or her national identity only through receiving the grant of citizenship from the state. There is an argument that the same process applies in the United Kingdom. It could be put forward that we are part of a British nation only by virtue of the fact that we are the legal subjects of the British Crown. In the USA the same would appear to apply. Americans become Americans through the adoption of citizenship of the United States, through obedience to the constitution of the United States and through loyalty to the flag of the United States. If it is true that it is only the authority of the existing state which confers our nationhood upon us, then the post-modernist intellectuals are right that as the enfeebled 'nation-state' decays, so too will nationhood.

But is that all nationhood really is? If it is, how can we explain the restless history of nations? Why do communities living within an existing state come to refuse to accept the legitimacy of the state which governs them and assert a rival nationhood? If it is the state which really does define and create national identity, why should Scottish people in the name of national identity come to reject a three hundred year old British state? Why should Catalans come to reject the Spanish state, Flemish the Belgian state and many Lombards the Italian state, not to speak of the wide range of nations of eastern Europe against whose aspirations for national identity and national self-determination the states of Yugoslavia, Czechoslovakia and the Soviet Union proved incapable of standing? Those states collapsed with hardly a whisper of communal or personal loyalty uttered in their support. No one would now speak of a Soviet nation or of a Yugoslav one. Events in Europe since 1989 have confirmed that a state by itself cannot create a nation. Real nations are not constructed by legislative enactment or by international treaty.

If a nation owes its creation to something other than the existence of a state, what is it which does give birth to nationhood? I have recently read a 'post-modern' interpretation of English national identity which did accept that there is more to nationhood than the mere willingness of citizens to accept the authority of a particular state.[2] It accepted that there is a type of customary thinking in a nation which characterises its essence. The writer then conducts his own investigation in order to discover the peculiar features of this customary thinking which go to construct our English nationhood. He claims success in his search, for he manages to locate our Englishness in an 'empirical approach' he dates back to the writings of John Locke. Our empiricism, apparently, is an unfortunate failing which he believes we ought to confront and overcome! He seems unaware that nineteenth century historians greatly exaggerated the influence of John Locke on his late seventeenth century contemporaries and on English thought in the half century which followed him.[3] Even if we leave this exaggeration to one side, I am not convinced by this definition of Englishness. We may possess an empirical, non-theoretical approach but is it peculiar to us? Post-modern theoreticians residing in universities may rant against a society which pays no attention to their jargon-filled tomes and they may dream that other countries possess more receptive audiences but I suspect that most people, wherever they may dwell, will base their judgement and reactions on empirical, pragmatic and rational scrutiny of experienced cause and effect – or at least they will assume that it is sensible to try to do so. They will only try not to act according to their own empirically based judgement if they are oppressed into behaving differently by some totalitarianism based on ideology or religion.

Hostility to totalitarianism perhaps is where instead we might identify a deep-rooted feature of our Englishness. We English have resisted totalitarianism earlier than most other peoples, doing so as early as the sixteenth century when we rejected the monolithic and avaricious Roman Church. We have opposed totalitarianism more fervently and more tenaciously than most other nations, as our twentieth century history has confirmed. Does that help provide us with a means of discovering the essence that defines our Englishness? Certainly we have rallied as a nation many times in the past against foreign enemies whose rule was characterised by authoritarianism and oppression. Before Hitler there was Napoleon and before Napoleon, Louis the 'Sun King'. This readiness to fight for our customary and individual freedom is an inescapable aspect for any study of our national history. The work of Linda Colley, on the forging of British nationhood in the eighteenth century, shows how under the inspiration of a sturdy Protestantism the English and Scottish peoples rallied in the military and ideological struggle against French absolutism.[4]

---

[2] Anthony Easthope, *Englishness and National Culture*, Routledge London 1999.

[3] For the argument that Locke's influnce has been exaggerated see J. C. D. Clark, *English Society 1688-1832*, 1985

[4] Linda Colley, *Britons: Forging the Nation*, Pimlico 1994. Colley argued that the long struggle against Bourbon, then Jacobin and then Bonapartist France was a key experience in forging a new nationhood. I do not find convincing her argument that a new British national identity emerged in the period. The encouragement of Britishness as an identity could only be effective because it was not replacing or subverting the old identity of Englishness but subsuming and incorporating it.

So in the search to define our nationhood we must seek the customs and political values we hold in common and distinguish those key ones which determine identity. In so doing we face the problem of distinguishing accurately between what are real determining qualities and what are only symptoms or reflections of a separate existence. George Orwell gave perhaps the most famous description of the defining features of Englishness in *The Lion and the Unicorn*.

> When you come back to England from any foreign country, you have immediately the sensation of breathing a different air. Even in the first few minutes dozens of small things conspire to give you this feeling. The beer is bitterer, the coins are heavier, the grass is greener, the advertisements are more blatant. The crowds in the big towns, with their mild knobbly faces, their bad teeth and gentle manners, are different from a European crowd. Then the vastness of England swallows you up, and you lose for a while your feeling that the whole nation has a single identifiable character. Are there really such things as nations? Are we not forty-six million individuals, all different? And the diversity of it, the chaos! The clatter of clogs in the Lancashire mill towns, the to-and-fro of the lorries on the Great North Road, the queues outside the Labour Exchanges, the rattle of pin-tables in the Soho pubs, the old maids biking to Holy Communion through the mists of the autumn morning – all these are not only fragments, but *characteristic* fragments, of the English scene. ... Yes, there *is* something distinctive and recognizable in English civilization. ... It is somehow bound up with solid breakfasts and gloomy Sundays, smoky towns and winding roads, green fields and red pillar-boxes. [5]

This reads somewhat uncertainly now. In fact, those customs and traits which Orwell identified in his time were really only contemporary and transitory symptoms of a nationhood whose distinct qualities were made much earlier. Symptoms can emerge, develop, change and disappear. We are not made into a nation just by the sharing of certain patterns of contemporary behaviour. We were not made into a nation in the sixties and seventies by the common experience of watching the same television programmes as some media commentators liked to imagine and assert. That shared cultural experience turned out to be a relatively brief one as the technology of mass entertainment moved on.

So it is not the experience of a common government by a single state and it is not the common acceptance of particular patterns of behaviour or of cultural and political norms which create, determine or decide what a nation is. These are symptoms only. Where should we look in our quest for the origins of our nationhood? Nations have to be sought in history – they are the fruits of processes lasting centuries, even millennia; they are the fruits of countless willed and unwilled acts that over time create distinct

---

[5] George Orwell, *Collected Essays Vol.2*, p75-76

communities of ethnicity, language, mentality, behaviour, memory and shared endeavour. They are not simple communities which can be shallowly defined by isolating just one of the aspects, say, that of language or of territory or of political tradition. Only by attempting to comprehend the whole complex of confused and confusing features, features that seem to change even as you look at them, can we hope to gain an understanding of the phenomenon of nationhood. After this is understood, when you identify yourself as English, you identify yourself with an unfolding process rather than with some static condition of being. For example I am ethnically English but that does not make me English in a full sense. I may have inherited some of my cultural attitudes, values and other traits from my English grandparents and parents and I may have shared common experiences in adulthood with the English community in which I have lived, but that still does not make me fully English. All these influences have helped to shape my own Englishness – but not fully, not so as to complete a process. There is always more of my Englishness for me to uncover and to understand.

There is the discovery of our literature, a body of writing barely bounded by the accepted content of the academic cannon, but enriched and enhanced by the distinctly English tradition of nature writing to be found in Gilbert White, Thomas Bewick, Francis Kilvert and W. H. Hudson, by the English tradition of writing about the condition of countryside life as in William Cobbett, Richard Jefferies and H. J. Massingham and by the English tradition of literature which counterposes natural and inherited living to the rootless destructiveness of a society in transition as in John Clare, Thomas Hardy and D. H. Lawrence. The list is hardly exhausted here and writers can be added to it, like Edward Thomas and Rudyard Kipling who could spin a sense of enchantment from a countryside which holds within it an ancient past. This literature may perhaps only provide a symptom of Englishness but through reading it and sharing the writer's emotions and loyalties we can come close to discovering the beating heart of the English soul. Then there is English music with the discovery of Elgar, of Delius, of Cecil Sharp, of Vaughan Williams and English painting with the discovery of Constable and Turner, English architecture with the discovery of Lutyens. Some of those names, like Thomas or Vaughan Williams, may suggest a non-English ethnicity but that became irrelevant as those individuals demonstrated a commitment to the revitalisation of a specifically English cultural tradition.

Once this diffuse and intangible essence of Englishness is understood, we can perceive just how nonsensical the claim was that our nationhood must perish with the apparent enfeebling and decomposition of the existing British state. The United Kingdom is not in truth a nation-state; it is a dynastic state, forcing together under its rule historically determined nations. The United Kingdom is not the only state which is a fraud when claiming the status of 'nation-state'. Indeed hardly any of the existing major states in Europe are true nation-states, created as the fulfilment of a process of national awakening. The Italian state was the creation of the House of Savoy and the Piedmontese conquest of other states in the mid nineteenth century; the German state was the creation of the Hohenzollerns and Prussian conquests of other states a little later. The wars of self-styled national unification which created Italy and Germany cut off awkward, indigestible sections of the ethnic nation (such as Trieste and Austria) while uniting the rest. As for France, Alexis de Tocqueville correctly observed that the French Republic is the descendant of the Bourbon dynastic state, whose frontiers Richelieu and Mazarin had pushed out into Flanders and Lotharingia, suppressing national identities as they did so. If the modern state is losing its legitimacy and is facing looming irrelevance, it is not the nation state that is on the way out but states whose character was formed as dynastic ones and which have masqueraded as nation-states ever since. If it is really true that we are on the point of living in a 'post-modern' age, this may be an age not when national identity will be discarded and forgotten, but one in which it may flourish freely throughout our continent as it has not for a thousand years. As one journalist has written; 'National loyalties cannot be eradicated; in the end the grass grows through the concrete.'[6] Shedding the shrivelling skin of the United Kingdom, the folk of England may step out into a freedom we have not known since the Norman conquerors took it from us nine hundred years ago.

Before we allow ourselves to rejoice in this happy image of the revival of true nationhood, there are qualifications which need to be made. Power may be moving away from states but into the grasp of larger supra-national bodies, not to smaller, more intimate and ancient ones. When our rulers reduce and subvert the sovereignty of existing states, they do not do so in order to restore decision-making to the dispossessed, but in order to organise their own escape from the restrictions which democratic practices have placed upon them. Democrats and radicals have secured, over the past two hundred years of campaigning, checks and balances within the familiar state structures designed to restrain the behaviour of the governing elites. When politicians agree to transfer sovereign powers to supra-national institutions over which democratic controls are tenuous, they threaten to diminish the effectiveness of these hard-won checks and balances. Government by international law reduces government by parliamentary statute allowing unaccountable, unelected and virtually unremovable members of the judiciary to purloin vital areas of decision-making from the political domain.[7] The will of the people is thereby replaced by the will of appeal courts. The vast geographical gap between rulers and ruled renders established democratic checks even weaker and easier to evade. The fate of democracy in a globalized world can already be seen in the United States where the very size of the country makes politics in Washington seem to many of its people irrelevant or impossible to influence. The result is a low rate of participation in federal elections. Transnational corporations also have much to gain from a world in which territorial states no longer have the power to restrict the industrial or commercial practices of

---

[6] William Rees-Mogg , article in *The Times* 1999, quoted in George Gardiner *A Bastard's Tale* p271.

[7] For fuller implications of the incorporation of supranational conventions, see John Tate, "Incorporating an Anathema: The unwarranted role of rights and the European Convention in UK law", *The European Journal*, November 1999.

corporations, even when their practices are ethically dubious, culturally destructive and environmentally dangerous. Corruption flourishes within vast supra-national institutions. The trend to globalism is too advantageous to the ruling elites for them ever to discard it unless they are forced to do so by a powerful movement of the disempowered.

If our nation is placed today upon a fragile pivot, swaying between rebirth and disintegration, the urgent question which faces us is how a movement of the dispossessed can be inspired to reclaim its lost culture, self-confidence and self-government? In a bewildering passage Linda Colley claims to believe that the British state was able to invigorate the loyalty of its subjects by playing upon the feeling that there existed outside the national community something which she calls 'the Other'. She argued that to the eighteenth century British, having adopted the Protestant world-view, this 'other' was Catholic and French. She wrote:

> A powerful and persistently threatening France became the haunting embodiment of that Catholic Other which Britons had been taught to fear since the Reformation in the sixteenth century. Confronting it encouraged them to bury their internal differences in the struggle for survival, victory and booty. 'There is no more effective way of bonding together the disparate sections of restless peoples', as Eric Hobsbawm has written, 'than to unite them against outsiders.' Imagining the French as their vile opposites, as Hyde to their Jekyll, became a way for Britons – particularly the poorer and less privileged – to contrive for themselves a converse and flattering identity.[8]

This passage smacks of the view that it is somehow unnatural for people to hold national loyalties and identities. It implies that a government must construct an outside 'Other' before the nation it leads can operate as one. It suggests that all national identity is somehow contrived and false or, if not false, it is based only on conflict and hostility and Colley is certainly convinced that the British state has been militaristic and aggressive. Yet why is it necessary that identity must be based upon finding a contrasting opposite or antagonist? In all of us we have several layers of identity – gender, family, local, ethnic, national, religious, political and linguistic. Sometimes these identities which we hold within our persons create stresses but for the bulk of our lives we contain these tensions and do not feel any condition of 'otherness' pushing its way between the different identities. Within the same person different identities can co-exist happily. There is no reason, therefore, why a sense of national identity should be based upon hatred or distaste for those who hold within themselves a different balance of identities. In fact a deepening awareness of our national togetherness can enrich our consciousness of our responsibilities and affiliation to larger identities as well as help to situate more local and more particular ones. In the past two hundred years it has not

---

[8] Linda Colley, *Britons: Forging the Nation*, p368, Pimlico 1994

been 'Little Englanders' who have dragged us into those wars which could and should have been avoided but the self-styled 'idealists' who have dreamed of cosmopolitan empires and cosmopolitan ideologies. Tony Blair's recent Kosovan adventure is just the latest example of how a commitment to overtly unselfish cosmopolitanism can plunge us into war when a realistic assessment of English national interest would have kept us at peace. The argument that national identity is an artificial construction which is only stirred into existence by stimulating hatred for others is an argument produced by those who loathe nationhood. It is an argument produced by, to quote Orwell again 'intellectuals ... ashamed of their own nationality.'

If an awareness of nationhood is not to be built by constructing an artificial 'Other', the question remains of how it is to be done? There is much reason for caution over this. Movements and organisations often do not turn out quite as we might expect. In the late 1970s Tom Nairn, in an interesting essay, *The English Enigma*, proposed that a 'left-nationalist popular culture' had begun to arise in England during the sixties and seventies. This, he observed, was 'progressive and generous'.[9] We must obviously wonder now where Nairn's progressive and generous popular culture was manifest and how we managed to miss it. Nairn located it in the 'History Workshop' movement.

> In the 1960s it expanded on to the scale of a national movement, above all through the influence of Raphael Samuel's 'History Workshops' in Ruskin College, Oxford. Expressed in the Workshop's *Journal* and many other publications, this seminal movement has fostered a new general culture and outlook to some extent balancing the simultaneous growth of sectarian Marxism in England.[10]

The only trouble with this charming view is that it seemed to have existed in Nairn's mind rather than in reality. When I visited 'History Workshops' in the seventies and eighties the mentality of the participants was hardly popular and not at all nationally minded. E. P. Thompson of all leftist intellectuals came closest to the image given by Nairn of a generous-hearted and determined democrat. He was a thinker and writer who was aware of his Englishness. He was also during the seventies the butt of polemics from the swarms of lesser minds who lacked his grandeur of vision and who preferred obscurantist – and now obsolete – 'Althusserian' discourse. Their Althusserian socialism led them to repudiate their Englishness, not to rejoice in it. I recall some time in the eighties a woman, who in a debate spoke from the floor and dared to expose her love of England, her Englishness and her lack of any sense of shame or embarrassment about our country's past. I looked for her at the end to

---

[9] One can then detect a much more concrete hope in the British political future. The latter depends mainly upon the English people. Here, in this progressive and generous cultural movement, they have at least part of what corresponds to the usual model of nationalist revival – the attempt to find strength for a better, more democratic future by re-examining ... a mythic past.' Tom Nairn, *The Break-Up of Britain*, Verso, 1981 p304.

[10] *ibid* p303

congratulate her on speaking out and it was clear from her warm reaction to my words that she felt just as beleaguered in the company which the 'History Workshop' provided as I did. As for the *History Workshop Journal,* this, even more than the conferences, reflected the sterile arrogance of the academy. Genuine popular culture was not present in it. Sadly Nairn was quite wrong about where we might find the roots of a renaissance in Englishness.

So where might we perceive signs that a sense of nationhood is not only surviving but reviving. A sense of English identity thrives on a delight in English landscape, on an awareness of English country, on a closeness to English earth. Here I perceive great hope. There are movements and organisations strengthening which do express a concern for, even a love for, our English soil. I see a remarkable growth of the ecological movement in England. For instance bodies like 'the National Trust', 'the Council for the Protection of Rural England', 'the Countryside Restoration Trust', 'Common Ground', 'the Woodland Trust', 'the Soil Association', 'Plantlife', the various county 'Wildlife Trusts' and 'the Royal Society for the Protection of Birds' have all grown dramatically in the past two decades both in membership and in vitality. The RSPB has topped a million while the National Trust topped two million early in the nineties and has gone on rising. Many years ago the Trust moved beyond a narrow concern with preserving stately homes and it is now a leading force within in the general environmental cause. As I write, I have before me a National Trust circular which urges me to donate to 'Operation Neptune', a project to acquire and so protect the most beautiful and vulnerable parts of our coastline. The campaign manager concludes:

> We are an island race. Every one of us has an affinity with the sea and a love of our coastline – no matter which part of it is precious to us as an individual. As a nation we have always defended it from enemies. Now it is time to defend it again.[11]

This is where our hope for the future lies. There is a movement among English people in which we seek to find our roots again in the countryside, in the woodlands, by the coastlines and beaches, along the hedgerows and in the meadows. It is partly unconscious, as many participants will not perceive it as overtly a national movement, but the emotional force behind it finds its source in a sense that the inheritance and identity of our nation is under threat. By campaigning to protect the integrity of the countryside, we feel we are striving to protect the integrity of the nation itself. If there is an 'Other' which provides an antagonist, it is not another nation but the spirit of globalism and irresponsible commercial greed. Here, within environmental and heritage campaigning, is to be found that generous and progressive movement which Tom Nairn wrongly thought he had found in a few Oxford seminars and conferences.

---

[11] Richard Offen, *Will You help us protect our beautiful coastline for ever?*, July 1999

Once we care for the land, we find ourselves asking questions about our national past. How has our land come to be so vulnerable to those who do not cherish her? The grief we feel now over the destruction of the landscape has been felt before. The poetry of John Clare in his lament over the enclosures of the early nineteenth century evokes the same sense of loss over the sacrifice of earthly beauty as we feel now over the loss of hedgerows, field ponds and orchards. This continuing sense of loss provides us with a national tradition, a continuing sense of deprivation from the full enjoyment of the land we have inherited as a people. We can travel back further in time in search of a folk tradition embedded in a yearning for the land. In 1649, in the years of turmoil at the end of the Civil War when radical change seemed possible, Gerrard Winstanley and a community of True Levellers or Diggers occupied and cultivated wasteland on St. George's Hill in Surrey. Winstanley's justification for his action was based on his interpretation of the consequences of the Norman Conquest.[12] Winstanley believed that the land of England belonged as of right to the English people but our ancestors had suffered from 'the Norman Yoke'. They had been subjected to foreign rule and denied ownership of their own land. This was a widely shared belief among his contemporaries. For instance in 1647 John Hare had written about the effects of the battle of Hastings:

> Is it tolerable ... that after such privileges conferred on us by heaven we should have our spirits so broken and un-Teutonised by one unfortunate battle as for above five hundred years ... to rest under the disgraceful title of a conquered nation and in captivity and vassalage to a foreign power? ... We cannot move but we hear the chains of our captivity rattle.[13]

When we investigate the political ideals at the time of English Civil War we find that the democratic Leveller movement was inspired by a belief that the English people were oppressed as a nation. The Levellers called for virtual manhood suffrage on the grounds that this was the ancient right of the English before the Norman Conquest had taken it away. The first democratic movement in England, therefore, was driven by a conviction that our nationhood was being suppressed. The Levellers did not share the contempt for Englishness of the twentieth-century left-wing intellectual. Instead they rejoiced in their Englishness and looked far back in time for the vindication of their programme. H. N. Brailsford, the historian of the Levellers, observed:

> When the Levellers invited the liberated descendants of the Anglo-Saxons to claim the proud status of equal citizens in a commonwealth, it was not to

---

[12] The main thing that you should look upon is the land, which calls upon her children to be freed from the entanglements of the Norman task-masters ... When William Duke of Normandy had conquered England, he took possession of the earth for his freedom and disposed of our English ground to his friends as he pleased, and made the conquered English his servants, to plant the earth for him and his friends'. Gerrard Winstanley, *An Appeal to the House of Commons Desiring their Answers* and *The Law of Freedom in a Platform*.

[13] H. N. Brailsford, *The Levellers and the English Revolution*, p141, 1961.

a perilous journey towards a remote and unhomely Utopia that they summoned their fellow countrymen They invited them to resume their 'native rights'.[14]

The struggle for our democracy began not as a relatively modern response to the experience of industrialization, not as a consequence of the ideas of the French Revolution, not as part of some international movement of human rights. The fight for English democracy began because manhood suffrage was perceived as an Englishman's right, an inheritance that was denied to us by the oppression of the Normans. Brailsford commented on one of the writings of John Lilburne, the most famous Leveller leader;

> In *Regal Tyranny Discovered* what he is really advocating is a return to the simplicity of Anglo-Saxon days ... His ideal was the 'Gemot' which used to decide everything once a month in every hundred. [15]

In the late eighteenth century the same approach appears in the writing of Major John Cartwright whose book of 1776 *Take Your Choice!* revived the call for manhood suffrage. Cartwright argued that in King Alfred's time England had been a customary democracy with a high-minded, benevolent and restrained prince to oversee it and maintain its principles. When he formed this interpretation of English history, Cartwright was influenced by the ideas that had been outlined in an earlier work, thought to have been written by Obadiah Hulme.[16] This influential essay resurrected the image of ancient Germany presented centuries before by the Roman writer Tacitus.

> It is reported by historians that our Saxon forefathers had no kings, in their own country, but lived in tribes or small communities, governed by laws of their own making and magistrates of their own electing. [17]

This assertion that there was a democratic government of England in Anglo-Saxon times was repeated throughout the decades which followed. It was the most popular vindication for democracy, seen as far more potent than the argument of the cosmopolitan radical, Tom Paine, that democracy was justified by the abstract 'rights of man'. Joseph Gerrald, for example, was arrested for speaking at a convention of democratic reformers in Edinburgh in late 1793. He was sentenced in a Scottish court to fourteen years transportation and died in Australia. In his Edinburgh speech he had celebrated 'the golden days' of King Alfred's time when 'the annual meeting of all freemen was an acknowledged part of our venerable constitution' and went on to

---

[14] *ibid* p536

[15] *ibid* p124

[16] *Historical Essay on the English Constitution*, 1771

[17] *ibid* p12

argue forcefully that democratic government was a right justified by its 'Gothic' or Anglo-Saxon origins.[18]

The search for our Englishness leads us into forgotten pathways. We discover that winning our democracy, of which we should all be proud, was not the result of struggles of an international labour movement as it is so often presented, but a specifically English concern, inspired by the sense of a lost English freedom. It is not true that our history has been a straightforward, progressive march to an enlightened future, emancipated from the constraints of a narrow national past. Instead the image of the past has guided our concerns, loyalties and desires. The image of Anglo-Saxon England which motivated that struggle for democracy may have been a romantic and distorted one. It may have been a dream, based on fairly spurious late mediaeval documents. But that did not undermine its potency to Englishmen intent on winning back what they perceived as the lost political inheritance of freedom. It was a dream acting through time to mould the aspirations of English people over generations. It was perhaps like 'the dreamtime' of the Australian Aborigines, an inspiring dream of origins, helping a dispossessed people to hold together and combine with an awareness of common identity and common purpose.

So this is where my search for Englishness has led – back into our Anglo-Saxon or Englisc past. Our Englisc past has the fascination of a period of time only partly known and still awaiting further discovery and interpretation but, even more importantly, it has the significance of a 'dreamtime' of our nation, the formative years of our values, attitudes and beliefs. The democratic campaigners of the 17th, 18th and 19th centuries may have exploited a distorted view of Englisc government and may have stressed a political egalitarianism which was not in fact as they imagined but there is enough in the pages of Tacitus to vindicate some of their dream. Perhaps we need such a dream now, a dream which, as in the ancient lines of the poem 'Widsið', leads us through the Germanic landscape of our past, revealing to us fragments of the tales of distant honour, courage and renown. If we seek for our Englishness and trace back our nationality through the leaves and branches of time, through the manifold patterns in our English landscape, our English country, our English earth, we follow our Englishness to its roots, to its Anglo-Saxonness, we then find no cause for that sniggering contempt of the intellectuals which so annoyed Orwell. Tacitus wrote of the Chauci who were probably the ancestors of a large fraction of the later Saxon confederation:

---

[18] 'Our rights have the two-fold sanction of reason and antiquity. We have seen, that the temple of British freedom is a Gothic fabric, which reared by the hands and cemented by the blood of our ancestors, is at once venerable for age, and respectable for utility. It is a structure which we can claim as an inheritance from our fathers, who claimed it themselves from the political patriarchs in the old time before them'. Joseph Gerrald, *Address of the British Convention assembled at Edinburgh, November 19, 1793 to the People of Great Britain*, 1793 p15.

They are the noblest people of Germany; one that prefers to maintain its greatness by honest dealing. Untouched by greed or lawless ambition, they live in quiet seclusion, never provoking a war, never robbing or plundering their neighbours. It is proof of their valour and strength that their superiority does not rest on aggression ... Their good-name stands as high in peace as in war. [19]

If that was 'the dreamtime' world of our Englishness, it is not a bad one to guide us now, as 'the dreamtime' world guides some Australian Aborigines, through all the confusion, corruption and dishonour of our present. .

---

[19] Tacitus, *Germania*.

On Being English in America:
A Personal Memoir

Gárman Lord

"Mommy, what nationality are we?"

Surely to almost any other ear but an American one, such a childish question would sound impossibly absurd. That it seems such a natural one in America, apt to be asked at some point in most any "American" (i.e., culturally assimilated) family, probably says more profound things to the rest of the world about what sort of country we are than could any amount of disquisitory prose by me or anyone else. If you are European, try to imagine what it must be like to live in a household where every child inevitably comes to ask, in his growing-up: "Mommy, what nationality are we?" and where such a question is quite taken for granted, and you will thereby tell yourself worlds about what it is like to call yourself "American".

At the very least, you will have told yourself that the answer is not inevitably "American" (though in certain jingoistic kinds of American families, such as hyper-enthusiastic newly naturalised immigrants, that answer may in fact sometimes be heard), which tells you further that not many Americans really think of American as a proper nationality. And that may tell you that, after in some cases a dozen or more generations in this country, it would seem that "folk roots" do indeed run remarkably deep.

Which is not to say, of course, that they may not also run quite gnarled and twisty, especially as they encounter hardpan, barren soil or stony historical vicissitudes of one kind or another. I vaguely recall putting that childish question to my own mother, when I was wee, and likewise at least the gist of what she answered. She said, without hesitation: Scotch, with some French, and a little bit of American Indian. I don't put this in quotes, mind you, because I am sure that is not exactly what she said. She may have mentioned other odd things, and in particular I seem to recall that she ventured a few fractional percentages, which may suggest that this was not the first time the question had ever come up in our family. But of course all this was at an age when fractional percentages would have been so much Hebrew to me; my mother, however, was and is a remarkably scrupulous sort of woman.

However, what else she was and is also bears noting in this context, namely, a fairly classic skinny blonde horsefaced giddy-brainy schoolmarmish Anglo-Saxon type, maiden name Smith, who probably could have just as easily fitted her natural prognathism around a plum, instead of an American twang, had that happened to be the character of the parlance learned at her own mother's knee. Today, then, the question of why she at no point in her iteration included "English," as my own adult perusal of the neglected subject of our real family tree would strongly suggest to have been better, has at least one rather interesting answer. It happens that she sprang of "ancient" New England Yankee farmer stock, including hordes of ancestors, two centuries and more agone, who were amongst that parcel of squirrel-hunters who abandoned their plows and axes and took up their arms in the cause of American Independence, an unpleasantness between our several nations the memory of which abides instinctively, albeit unconsciously, in her familial memory to this very day. For her, and some of her line still living, there exists an imaginary squirrel-gun hung on a rude imaginary back-country mantelpiece, with imaginary powder and shot not far to seek, against the prospect that that imaginary lobsterback "redcoat" King's soldiery should return and have to be fought and sniped and resisted again, at Lexington, Concord, Valley Forge and all those blood-gory storied places the family's ancestral fetch still so vividly remembers. I knew my own Great Grandmother Stewart, who grew up at the knee of her own Grandmother "Burpee" (Burkby), who was the daughter of a Revolutionary Soldier who marched off to war against Mad King George with George Washington and Paul Revere, and certainly knew all the war-stories. In other words, a living memory-bridge; folk memory of trauma, like folk roots, also lives on long and long.

However, I had to grow up and think about things myself to understand this dynamic, a folk mechanism that I think is not well-understood by anybody else but me in my own family, or amongst anyone of that stock I still know, to this day. (America is a big country, and we have all since got around.) Family is like the air we breathe all unaware; so usual that I think perhaps nobody before me has ever noticed quite an odd thing; namely, that while American Revolutionary ancestry is about the closest thing that America has to an "aristocracy", nonetheless none of these families of that high-born ilk ever seem to call themselves the thing that they most patently are: English. Scots, French, Indian, almost anything but English, harking back to a day when America obviously yearned so desperately for some identity of its own quite averse, by the political correctness of the time, to identifying in any way with the national identity of the foe. Empire, Commonwealth, call it what you will, the American-English of those days did not think of themselves as rebelling against the "British" crown, they quite patently, and this from my own familial memory, thought of themselves as fighting against the "English" crown. Today, in fact, any time an American is heard to call himself "English", it's a dead giveaway that he is of some more recent English ilk than Revolutionary.

An example is an old drinking pal of mine who would readily call himself "English", though his father was indeed of the same old line Yankee Revolutionary stock as myself. His mother, however, who was the more influential in his formative life, happened to have been an English war-bride from WWII, in relative terms "just off the boat," and with no reason to call herself anything else but English. And still, it is worth mentioning, with her public school accent intact. I knew the family quite well, and she and I had many an interesting chat, since she had come in her old age to be somewhat keener on the subject of English history, at least for conversation's sake, a subject I seemed to know considerably more about than she did. (As she used to say, for us it's King Arthur, and then the Battle of Hastings, and in between, well, nothing, really.) Quite often I would get a giggle out of her ("Oh, it's YOU!!") by answering her phone calls in an imitation of her own accent, which I am sure she maintained for so many decades even on these shores with some calculation. In America, where really old authentic pioneering English families never admit they are English, an English accent, even English blood, bears nonetheless a very considerable social cachet; pretty little Betty Waterbury must have noted the strength of that immediately upon her arrival here, and would obviously have been mad to give it up in trade for a phony acquired American twang. It is all quite characteristic of the many absurdities involved in the through-the-looking-glass conundrum of being "American", especially "Anglo-American". In this "nation" of immigrants, almost any other accent you might have you do well to lose as soon as possible, in favor of sounding more "American;" talk English, Papa, you're in America now! The exception to the rule is an English accent, which he who has it, if it is a good one, may do better socially to keep, and which some individuals whom no one would by any stretch of the imagination call "Anglo-Saxon" in appearance, nonetheless are sometimes seen to cultivate as an affectation.

As to my mother, well, she was not entirely wrong, just rather notably incomplete, for the most "American" of reasons. It was true enough that there was an Indian in there somewhere, though my own genealogical researches have yet to identify him; some Frenchmen too, from nearby Canada, and certainly true that any number of Scotsmen, called "Scotch-Irish," Stewarts, Munroes, MacPhersons, outlaws from seventeenth century British Isles religious jihads, only too anxious to transfer their seditions against the English King to his colonies on these shores, came here to Appalachia to contribute to my own ancestry, to the point where, from King George's point of view, the trouble with Appalachia is that it is full of Scots. However, that was then, and this is now...

Somewhere in the course of the historical vicissitudes of this "nation of immigrants", as it began to fill itself up with foreign cheap labor, a subtle shift in consciousness amongst the old stock, born of xenophobic anxiety, began to move from how English you aren't to how English you are, although you never called it "English," but more usually "Anglo-Saxon." Here was the point at which "Englishness," becoming a little scarcer, began to acquire the livery of some sort of American "aristocracy". Interestingly, it was never stated, so far as I know, in so many words; there just began to be a low-grade Romantic folk enthusiasm about the virtues of "Anglo-Saxon" culture that seeped its way into the arts and literature of, especially, the early twentieth century. No one noted any particular absurdity in regarding as "aristocratic" the sons of squirrel-hunters and hardscrabble farmers; it was the "Anglo-Saxon-ness" of the idea that counted. How Norman-luxurious and cultivated were Alfred's hall thanes, after all? It was still possible in those days to maintain the reification of the "noble savage", especially if he was a certifiably Anglo-Saxon savage. Moreover, despite their republican leveler notions, a good quarter of those English religious refugees who founded this country, including my own ancestors, were technically armigerous back in the British Isles, whether they brought any college of heraldry here with them or not.

Such was the lingering Low-Romantic school of the more Tory kind of old-blood American social thought right up to the middle of the present century, and in fact one still finds the occasional resonance of it to this day, though not echoing very loudly anymore. We English-Americans, when we do chance to meet in the midst of the madding McCulture, still know each other on sight, and, in our own circles, tend instinctively to switch to the old rules of engagement which nobody but ourselves understands. In my own days, in High School, I recall that a very odd thing happened to me. I had no sooner matriculated than I happened to write something for my new school's student paper, whereupon I found myself laid claim to by a certain English teacher, a Mrs. Stafford, who wanted me particularly in her class, and managed to keep me in her class, and keep me writing, my whole three years in attendance there.

Mrs. Stafford was really quite a wonderful woman in her way, little enough though I appreciated her, rather noble of feature. She was an enthusiast of literature, especially English literature, none of which enthusiasm ever did seep down to me, but she certainly tried. It seemed she had decided I could write, but none of that seeped down to me either; I was in fact resistive, passive-aggressive and resentful of all the attention, generally. I must surely have been one of her greatest pedagogic failures in life. I did write upon demand of course, whatever sort of thing she asked me to write, being boundlessly imaginative in those callow days, and rather enjoyed it, in its way, and that literary half-a-loaf output seemed enough to satisfy Mrs. Stafford too. She regularly filled up the student periodicals with my stuff, to the point where I gradually developed an unlooked-for student fan club of the nicer sort of kids, not all of them English stock, yet who actually seemed to applaud her taste and quite enjoyed reading me, much to my own puzzlement, since I myself never cared to read anything at all and spent every possible moment generally running wild.

It must be understood by those who have never been there that American public schools are very rough places, especially with the ambient secret undercurrents of ethnic chaos so peculiar to this country. I utterly hated school; I was a schoolyard tough and a thorogoing thug, affectedly and perfectly antisocial, as nasty as the best or worst of them in a schoolyard fistfight, which schoolyards, in my memory, were always veritable mediaeval Icelands. I hated all that, and I hated the school that spawned and fostered it. There was nothing that decently could be done with such a lot as me, at least not then, but Mrs. Stafford tried. In its way, that did affect me, and one thing that she did say ended up sticking with me forever. There was a day when she asked the class to raise their hands as to what ethnicity we were, and of course we all took our turns, I don't recall what I may have said I was; then after class Mrs. Stafford took me aside, over one of my assigned essay compositions, and asked me whether I might be English. Under the circumstances, old family superstitions notwithstanding, it did seem safe to admit that I was, whereupon she began to show me certain things she had remarked in my writing. My prose, so she said, was almost poetry, though in some ancient way. Particularly, she showed me the rythms and strings of alliterations, all unconscious with me of course, and asked if I knew who the Anglo-Saxons were. I naturally pretended I did, in hopes of getting out of there that much quicker, and left Mrs. Stafford suitably pleased with how much she was convinced she must have taught me, myself even more pleased to finally be going my ways. And I would have forgotten about it, except that, strangely, I found that I couldn't, and haven't been able to this day. Something in it all mystified me, intrigued me, in spite of what I childishly fancied my better self. Little as I cared about it, I could nonetheless never put it completely away from me, simply because I sensed some great riddle in it all and happened to have a child's prehensile mind.

Today, with all the riddles long solved, I have to admit, somewhat ruefully and after she is long dead and no longer worldly reachable, that Mrs. Stafford, all undreamed of at the time, turned out to be one of the most mysteriously lasting influences upon my life and thinking, just by virtue of those few words of hers that I ever actually bothered to listen to and remember, and what my later thinking ended up making of them over time. To this day, the mysterious "Mrs. Stafford" (her first name turned out to be Jean, or perhaps Jeanne) haunts my thoughts with a ghost, a folk fetch, if you will, that will not down.

In a larger sense, despite all our vast American resources and advantages, there is always a certain rootless angst about being an American, English-American or otherwise. In fact, America's original destiny, whatever we may want to call it, seems something quite unrecoverable, perhaps because it was never sound enough workmanship to begin with. To actually recover the old "English America" today, if one may be pardoned for what must seem like impossibly radical talk, would involve the creation of at least a quasi-English folk enclave on some part of the ground that was once called America at some future point after what we now call America shall be gone. One is not necessarily saying that one knows America will be gone in one's own lifetime. One merely notes that doomed empires do pass, and that our American one does look between the eyes to be pretty well doomed, even now in its full ramp, at least to me, and perhaps a few other Old Testamental prophet-types. Unlike so many others, I see us as falling, and even the exact way in which we are falling, with a good deal of precision. In that context, the only thing one could ever really do would be to plant the seeds of our next dispensation, if it all comes down in our lifetime, and simply hope for the best.

In an Englishman's visit to America, at least in the outback where I live, he undoubtably would see a lot of Americans who are of identifiably English stock, whether significantly aware of it or not, who, until they spoke up, might not look too out of place in an English country local. However, where I live is an American backwater, and vast tracts of this vast country, especially areas where the mainstream action of America is supposedly happening, don't really look like this at all. Queens, Long Island, for instance, where I just visited an old-line Irish friend, and decidedly one of America's busier places, undoubtedly would look to a visiting Englishman more like modern London, and most of the commercial signs in Dan O'Halloran's ancient storied neighborhood were in fact unreadable by either Dan or myself. They are in Korean, and Dan, with three university degrees, is obviously a foreigner, illiterate in the local language, in the neighborhood of his birth. Likewise America's capital city, Washington DC, where all our earth-shaking decisions on what stranger's country we shall smart-bomb today for no reason he could possibly be expected to understand are made, is only tenuously inhabited by the minor enclave of representatives we send there to govern us. The same sort of picture holds true as the reality across this ill-favored land, and the five huge states of the great American south-west, for instance, all the way from Galveston to Los Angeles, are today at least as Mexican as they were before the Mexican War, wherever they are not still Indian.

It's true enough that if I go travelling the length and breadth of this country, as I did last year, about all I ever see are white, often as not English, faces, and people with whom I can comfortably converse, being enough of a linguist, in a language most of our people have been speaking back to when it was first invented, no matter how thick the regional twang. However, where I go I do not go as a tourist; I know this country like a cat knows its scratch, and normally know where I am going and whom I am seeing there and why. And I also know that in so doing I am not seeing or dealing with the "real" America, much of which would hardly even be intelligible to me. Should I ever get lost somewhere in this vast land, chances are that I wouldn't even be able to ask the real locals for directions. I and all my kind know perfectly well that what we are living in is a false America, the facade of what is taken to be America and the pose she still strikes in the world at large, for practical exploitative purposes. But that of course is one of the fatal flaws in our Empire's makeup that I noted above, which tells the far-enough sighted that such a contraption cannot be sustained forever and must inevitably fall. The Patricians always pass, and it is the Plebeians, ex-slaves and such, that end up inheriting the imponderable future's Dark Ages.

As to that real America, what it would seem much more like to our visiting Englishman, if he got around in enough of it, would be an India, and in the end no one could any more make another England out of it than out of India. What I and my kind are in this country is not even a Brahmin class, though it is sometimes colloquially called that; in fact we are actually colonial sahibs in our own country, and these days everybody of all American classes seems to know it. And more and more, we ourselves feel it; very much strangers in our own land. It is a tremendously uncomfortable feeling, an angst. And in the midst of such discomfort our visiting Englishman would be puzzled to note how attenuated the sense of "Englishness" would seem, amongst, say, English stock workmates of mine in my workaday middle-class job. Our American-Englishmen, around here mostly the same stock as me, can't feel very English because for generations they have been taught not to; we are supposed to have left all that behind in the Revolution and gone on to create a whole new clean-slate dispensation, free of all the decadent vices of our European past, which supposedly we can't possibly go back to. But of course that never really works, and today we are none too sure that the historical bargain we bought into has turned out to be anything at all like we expected; we simply look round us now, at the real America we have accidentally created, and are left with a queasy sensation of being neither fish nor fowl here. Meanwhile, we have moreover that sense of being a somehow privileged sahib-class, which has its own guilty feeling about it. Under those circumstances, to answer to our new anomie by falling back upon our "Englishness" would only aggravate that guilty feeling, putting us at one more remove, and make it horribly worse.

These are the kinds of things that I see, as one of those rare Americans far-sighted enough to see through us and all our guff and bold enough to look, right clear through to the bottom line, and describe what I see. Others of my ilk don't see it, at least not yet, and in fact are apt to react resentfully to me when I try to point it out to them with all my Cassandra-philosophies. It isn't that they so much doubt it, as resent having it pointed out and rubbed in that much sorer, especially by some Chicken-Little who was really originally hired for a Map-Maker. Rather, they really don't want to see it. They may even consider it dangerous to themselves to see it; that's just human nature. It's just all too far from everything they were brought up believing for them to bear thinking about. To many of them, in fact, especially the less naturally big-brained ones, I must seem at least vaguely treasonous or seditious, perhaps even mad. To me, then, this, my normal workday, serves as an epitome of the fundamental, and I think ultimately fatal, American dilemma.

The catch in it all is that in America, to this day, as noted, a certain cachet goes with being "English", especially English of old colonial/Revolutionary stock, that founded all this. Yet on the other hand, much of that history is these days too "Eurocentric" to be taught to kids in most of our schools. But in fact it can't just be wished away, and looms that much larger in the minds of the non-English Americans the less they know about it. Whenever you have occasion to tell an American of color that your ethnicity is English, you can see a momentary impenetrable cloud pass over his gaze, of some strange thing between admiration and fear. This is really very awkward, I must say, since we are all constantly nagged and harangued by our culture that in America race is supposed to mean nothing, and yet you can see so plainly, though he doesn't say a word, that it obviously means a great deal to him. The impression given to most Americans of the kind our visiting Englishman meets here is that we are really sitting on a keg of dynamite that might take no more than a spark to set off, and in fact I'm sure we are. The new "average American" is to us already a stranger. We cannot read the stranger's eyes/ we cannot know his mood/ nor when his foreign gods may rise/ and repossess his blood. Notwithstanding, ordinary Americans of every polkadot color and stripe, unless they are hardcore ethnic radicals, always seem helplessly fascinated in the grip of the mystique of anything "English," for reasons that they may well understand better than we do who are blood-English and may take such things so much more for granted. There seems for them something about it all that smacks magically and romantically of Avalon. Yet that doesn't necessarily mean that there is anything in all that mystique that could somehow be worked with, to solve our "national" dilemma; in fact, more likely quite the reverse. Even a Welshman must die to get to Avalon, after all. Such mystique can no more than add pique and poignancy to the soul-pain of our general national angst.

The fundamental problem is that this country has never been authentically English, all the way back to the Revolution and before; it only thought it was, because its population of that time were all of that stock. In fact, by then, just like England and Europe, we were already starting to undergo a far more important Revolution, the Industrial Revolution, which set a fatal course for all of us. It meant the importation of cheap labor, from any place in the world we could get it, of a huge new plebian workforce far outnumbering the patrician old-blood class who owned them and their livelihoods, and of course, historically, it is always the patrician class, with everything to lose, which withers and falters in its vicissitudes, and the plebian class, with nothing to lose, which rises. By that time we were already casting about for some new philosophy to reassure us, in ways which the old inherited world view never could, in these new historical directions we were undertaking. Under the looming Faustian curse of America's traditional Puritanical Utopian streak, we seemed to become a nation of sociological mad scientists, casting about amongst such popinjay ideologies as international Romanticism, French Rationalism, Progressivism and Enlightenment philosophies, suppositiously more useful as new theses for our new "national" dispensation and manifest destiny, against which our old "Englishness" could only come to seem reactionary and treasonous. In that sense, we were already ideologically divorced from England long before the Boston Tea Party, and the American War of Independence, complete with French complicity, was only putting paid to the historical note. By Independence, all that was left of England amongst us was the commonplace stuff of life; the language, the folkways, the common law, the brain synapses, the air-we-breathe stuff that keeps up because no one can conceive of what to replace it with or how to do so. However, all that sort of thing is always local; nationally and internationally, ourselves and England, with just too much ocean between us, had long been going our separate ways, which was all that made Revolution possible in the first place.

This is the sort of thing that makes "Englishness", in our new dire straits, far too tenuous a model from the outset to ever consider reverting to nationally, in any meaningful way. Rather, American pundits seem to like to say, with almost a certain Progressivist pride, that America "keeps reinventing itself." It is uncanny how they never go on to say what would seem obvious to almost anyone but an American pundit; namely, how that must surely mean that we didn't get it right the first time, and still have never got it right yet. Rather, we have lived and dreamed on for hundreds of years now, insulated between two great oceans in a world of unworldly unreality, and it seems only a matter of time before we have to start thinking seriously about really reinventing ourselves, not dilitantishly like the pundits, but in some real way all too dire. That is the inevitable doomsday a-coming that I think people like me must be at least spiritually girded up and ready for.

Somewhere between Mrs. Stafford and 1976, I began to worry more and more about whether there was really anything to the elusive concept of America after all. We were never a folk, in the historical European sense, because we never troubled to become one, in the heady founding days, when Enlightenment philosophers imagined that mass public education would prove to be the cure for all of man's wrongs and society's ills, and hillbilly considerations such as folkdom seemed utterly unimportant. Instead, we went for mass cheap labor and a specious notion of "Pluralism;" import them, mass educate them, make good little Americans out of them, and presto, within three generations that would be that. But of course that wasn't that, not even close, and none of our elder geniuses in knee knickers, powdered wigs and three cornered hats ever really thought the great social experiment through, as to what in the world we would do if that somehow proved not to be that. Rather, they wrote us a Constitution, on foolscap, full of S's that look like F's, which is what we are now stuck with today in all its painful obsolescence all the way back to the War Between the States. Can we now get out from under that, then, and write ourselves a new modern one? In a country, mind you, which no longer exhibits any shared cultural vision, no longer teaches our real history in its schools because our real history's "Eurocentricity" would be too offensive to some other perfectly good Americans, nor is anyone even sure anymore exactly what an "American" is? Again, no, not even close. As one "Anglo-American" friend and colleague once put it to me, if we tried to draft a Constitution today, it would take ten years, cost ten billion dollars, and produce a document that would look like the Environmental Impact Statement for the Alaska Oil Pipeline. So much for any workable contemporary "American model" of nationality. It doesn't, nor can it, exist, but that's not the real tragedy. The real tragedy is how many of our best people still believe in quiet poltroon-desperation that the Emperor's New Clothes of our American Imperial model really do, somehow, still exist and cover our nakedness.

As for me, if I have to discard the now so long established but increasingly less workable obsolete "American" model somewhere along the way, that doesn't complicate my affairs but rather simplifies them. Since 1976 I have been guided in all aspects of my life by the values and outlook of the pre-Christian Anglo-Saxon folk religion. As what must seem, baldly so stated, an impossibly acrobatic backflip across time and the soaring arches of "civic-society" metaculture, such model may sound worse than no answer at all, yet strangely, for me at least, it has functioned very cleanly and well. The American model, which held up as long as it did, was always in its way at least as great a fraud as the Donation of Constantine, and not having to support it, going back rather to the surely no more fraudulent idea of being a mere "tribesman," frees me at long last from the insupportable burden of having to be a "sahib." Admittedly that all seems to throw the whole future up for grabs, but then, it also plays to my own personal strengths, and it seems to me that if the whole picture is as grim as I have been painting it, I'll do well to give myself every advantage I think I can get!

As to the plight of my country, and its likely prospects, the same pundits who like to point out that America keeps reinventing itself are just as fond of referring to us as a "nation of immigrants," blithely forgetting that not all of us came here as immigrants. Some of us, after all, came here as land-takers and conquerors. Likewise the notion of perpetual reinvention; such a perpetual agony does not, after all, so much actually reinvent anything as imperfectly overwrite one reification of ourselves with some other currently more convenient one; but a reification is still just a reification, with one reification hardly of more inherent worth than another. That being the case, there is surely nothing to stop me from replacing someone else's reification with my own preferred one. Dare to think big! And while you are doing so, note that every one of those four words is pure Anglo-Saxon!

First Steps in Old English
An easy to follow language course for the beginner

Stephen Pollington

A complete, well presented and easy to use Old English language course that contains all the exercises and texts needed to learn Old English. This course has been designed to be of help to a wide range of students, from those who are teaching themselves at home, to undergraduates who are learning Old English as part of their English degree course. The author is aware that some individuals have little aptitude for learning languages and that many have difficulty with grammar. To help overcome these problems he has adopted a step by step approach that enables students of differing abilities to advance at their own pace. The course includes exercises to test the students progress. A correspondence course is also available.

£19   ISBN 1–898281–19–X 250mm x 175mm/10" x 7"   224 pages

Ærgeweorc: Old English Verse and Prose

read by Stephen Pollington

This audiotape cassette can be used with *First Steps in Old English* or just listened to for the sheer pleasure of hearing Old English spoken well.

Tracks: 1. Deor. 2. Beowulf – The Funeral of Scyld Scefing. 3. Engla Tocyme (The Arrival of the English). 4. Ines Domas. Two Extracts from the Laws of King Ine. 5. Deniga Hergung (The Danes' Harrying) Anglo-Saxon Chronicle Entry AD997. 6. Durham 7. The Ordeal (Be ðon ðe ordales weddigaþ) 8. Wið Dweorh (Against a Dwarf) 9. Wið Wennum (Against Wens) 10. Wið Wæterælfadle (Against Waterelf Sickness) 11. The Nine Herbs Charm 12. Læcedomas (Leechdoms) 13. Beowulf's Greeting 14. The Battle of Brunanburh 15. Blacmon – by Adrian Pilgrim.

£7·50   ISBN 1–898281–20–3   C40 audiotape

Wordcraft: Concise English/Old English Dictionary and Thesaurus

Stephen Pollington

This book provides Old English equivalents to the commoner modern words in both dictionary and thesaurus formats. The Thesaurus presents vocabulary relevant to a wide range of individual topics in alphabetical lists, thus making it easily accessible to those with specific areas of interest. Each thematic listing is encoded for cross-reference from the Dictionary. The two sections will be of invaluable assistance to students of the language, as well as to those with either a general or a specific interest in the Anglo-Saxon period.

£11·95 A5 ISBN 1–898281–02–5 256pp

An Introduction to the Old English Language and its Literature

Stephen Pollington

The purpose of this general introduction to Old English is not to deal with the teaching of Old English but to dispel some misconceptions about the language and to give an outline of its structure and its literature. Some basic knowledge of these is essential to an understanding of the early period of English history and the present form of the language.

£4·95 A5 ISBN 1–898281–06–8 48pp

An Introduction to Early English Law

Bill Griffiths

Much of Anglo-Saxon life followed a traditional pattern, of custom, and of dependence on kin-groups for land, support and security. The Viking incursions of the ninth century and the reconquest of the north that followed both disturbed this pattern and led to a new emphasis on centralized power and law, with royal and ecclesiastical officials prominent as arbitrators and settlers of disputes. The diversity and development of early English law is sampled here by selecting several law-codes to be read in translation – that of Æthelbert of Kent, being the first to be issued in England, Alfred the Great's, the most clearly thought-out of all, and short codes from the reigns of Edmund and Æthelred the Unready.

£6·95 A5 ISBN 1–898281–14–9 96pp

The Battle of Maldon: Text and Translation

Edited and translated by Bill Griffiths

The Battle of Maldon was fought between the men of Essex and the Vikings in AD 991. The action was captured in an Anglo-Saxon poem whose vividness and heroic spirit has fascinated readers and scholars for generations. *The Battle of Maldon* includes the source text; edited text; parallel literal translation; verse translation; a review of 103 books and articles. This new edition has a helpful guide to Old English verse.

£6·95 A5 ISBN 0–9516209–0–8 96pp

Beowulf: Text and Translation

Translated by John Porter

The verse in which the story unfolds is, by common consent, the finest writing surviving in Old English, a text that all students of the language and many general readers will want to tackle in the original form. To aid understanding of the Old English, a literal word-by-word translation is printed opposite the edited text and provides a practical key to this Anglo-Saxon masterpiece.

£7·95   A5   ISBN 0–9516209–2–4   192pp

The English Warrior from earliest times to 1066

Stephen Pollington

This important new work is not intended to be a bald listing of the battles and campaigns from the Anglo-Saxon Chronicle and other sources, but rather it is an attempt to get below the surface of Anglo-Saxon warriorhood and to investigate the rites, social attitudes, mentality and mythology of the warfare of those times.

The book is divided into three main sections which deal with warriorhood, weaponry and warfare respectively. The first covers the warrior's role in early English society, his rights and duties, the important rituals of feasting, gift-giving and duelling, and the local and national military organizations. The second part discusses the various weapons and items of military equipment which are known to have been in use during the period, often with a concise summary of the generally accepted typology for the many kinds of military hardware. In the third part, the social and legal nature of warfare is presented, as well as details of strategy and tactics, military buildings and earthworks, and the use of supply trains. Valuable appendices offer original translations of the three principal Old English military poems, the battles of *Maldon*, *Finnsburh* and *Brunanburh*.

The latest thinking from many disciplines is brought together in a unique and fascinating survey of the role of the military in Anglo-Saxon England. The author combines original translations from the Old English and Old Norse source documents with archaeological and linguistic evidence to present a comprehensive and wide-ranging treatment of the subject. Students of military history will find here a wealth of new insights into a neglected period of English history.

£14·95   ISBN 1–898281–10–6   272pp   10" x 7" (250 x 175mm) with over 50 illustrations

A Handbook of Anglo-Saxon Food:
Processing and Consumption

Ann Hagen

For the first time information from various sources has been brought together in order to build up a picture of how food was grown, conserved, prepared and eaten during the period from the beginning of the 5th century to the 11th century. Many people will find it fascinating for the views it gives of an important aspect of Anglo-Saxon life and culture. In addition to Anglo-Saxon England the Celtic west of Britain is also covered. Now with an extensive index.

£8·95   A5   ISBN 0–9516209–8–3   192pp

A Second Handbook of Anglo-Saxon Food & Drink:
Production and Distribution

Ann Hagen

Food production for home consumption was the basis of economic activity throughout the Anglo-Saxon period. This second handbook complements the first and brings together a vast amount of information on livestock, cereal and vegetable crops, fish, honey and fermented drinks. Related subjects such as hospitality, charity and drunkenness are also dealt with. There is an extensive index.

£14·95   A5   ISBN 1–898281–12–2   432pp

English Heroic Legends

Kathleen Herbert

The author has taken the skeletons of ancient Germanic legends about great kings, queens and heroes, and put flesh on them. Kathleen Herbert's extensive knowledge of the period is reflected in the wealth of detail she brings to these tales of adventure, passion, bloodshed and magic.

The book is in two parts. First are the stories that originate deep in the past, yet because they have not been hackneyed, they are still strange and enchanting. After that there is a selection of the source material, with information about where it can be found and some discussion about how it can be used.

This title was previously published as *Spellcraft: Old English Heroic Legends*.

£11·95   A5   ISBN 1–898281–25–4   292pp

Peace-Weavers and Shield-Maidens: Women in Early English Society

Kathleen Herbert

The recorded history of the English people did not start in 1066 as popularly believed but one-thousand years earlier. The Roman historian Cornelius Tacitus noted in *Germania*, published in the year 98, that the English (Latin *Anglii*), who lived in the southern part of the Jutland peninsula, were members of an alliance of Goddess-worshippers. The author has taken that as an appropriate opening to an account of the earliest Englishwomen, the part they played in the making of England, what they did in peace and war, the impressions they left in Britain and on the continent, how they were recorded in the chronicles, how they come alive in heroic verse and jokes.

£4·95   A5   ISBN 1–898281–11–4   64pp

Looking for the Lost Gods of England

Kathleen Herbert

Kathleen Herbert sifts through the royal genealogies, charms, verse and other sources to find clues to the names and attributes of the Gods and Goddesses of the early English. The earliest account of English heathen practices reveals that they worshipped the Earth Mother and called her Nerthus. The tales, beliefs and traditions of that time are still with us and have played a part in giving us *A Midsummer Night's Dream* and *The Lord of the Rings*.

£4·95   A5   ISBN 1–898281–04–1   64pp

Rudiments of Runelore

Stephen Pollington

This book provides both a comprehensive introduction for those coming to the subject for the first time, and a handy and inexpensive reference work for those with some knowledge of the subject. The *Abecedarium Nordmannicum* and the English, Norwegian and Icelandic rune poems are included in their original and translated form. Also included is work on the three Brandon runic inscriptions and the Norfolk 'Tiw' runes.

£5·95   A5   ISBN 1–898281–16–5   Illustrations   88pp

English Martial Arts

Terry Brown

By the sixteenth century English martial artists had a governing body that controlled its members in much the same way as do modern-day martial arts organisations. The *Company of Maisters* taught and practised a fighting system that ranks as high in terms of effectiveness and pedigree as any in the world.

In the first part of the book the author investigates the weapons, history and development of the English fighting system and looks at some of the attitudes, beliefs and social pressures that helped mould it.

Part two deals with English fighting techniques drawn from sources that recorded the system at various stages in its history. In other words, all of the methods and techniques shown in this book are authentic and have not been created by the author. The theories that underlie the system are explained in a chapter on *The Principles of True Fighting*. All of the techniques covered are illustrated with photographs and accompanied by instructions. Techniques included are for bare-fist fighting, broadsword, quarterstaff, bill, sword and buckler, sword and dagger.

£25 ISBN 1–898281–18–1 250mm x 195mm /10" x 7½" 220 photographs 240 pages

The Hallowing of England
A Guide to the Saints of Old England and their Places of Pilgrimage

Fr. Andrew Phillips

In the Old English period we can count over 300 saints, yet today their names and exploits are largely unknown. They are part of a forgotten England which, though it lies deep in the past, is an important part of our national and spiritual history. This guide includes a list of saints, an alphabetical list of places with which they are associated, and a calendar of saint's feast days.

£5·95 A5 ISBN 1–898281–08–4 96pp

The Rebirth of England and English: The Vision of William Barnes

Fr. Andrew Phillips

English history is patterned with spirits so bright that they broke through convention and saw another England. Such was the case of the Dorset poet, William Barnes (1801–86), priest, poet, teacher, self-taught polymath, linguist extraordinary and that rare thing – a man of vision. In this work the author looks at that vision, a vision at once of Religion, Nature, Art, Marriage, Society, Economics, Politics and Language. He writes: 'In search of authentic English roots and values, our post-industrial society may well have much to learn from Barnes'.

£9·95 A5 ISBN 1–898281–17–3 160pp

Dark Age Naval Power
A Reassessment of Frankish and Anglo-Saxon Seafaring Activity
John Haywood

In the first edition of this work, published in 1991, John Haywood argued that the capabilities of the pre-Viking Germanic seafarers had been greatly underestimated. Since that time, his reassessment of Frankish and Anglo-Saxon shipbuilding and seafaring has been widely praised and accepted.

'The book remains a historical study of the first order. It is required reading for our seminar on medieval seafaring at Texas A & M University and is essential reading for anyone interested in the subject.'

F. H. Van Doorninck, *The American Neptune* (1994)

'The author has done a fine job, and his clear and strongly put theories will hopefully further the discussion of this important part of European history.'

Arne Emil Christensen, *The International Journal of Nautical Archaeology* (1992)

'Writing a comprehensive history of the clandestine activities of preliterate Dark Age societies is an ambitious task and this book is a remarkable achievement.'

Gillian Hutchinson, *Mariner's Mirror* (1993)

In this second edition, some sections of the book have been revised and updated to include information gained from excavations and sea trials with sailing replicas of early ships. The new evidence supports the author's argument that early Germanic shipbuilding and seafaring skills were far more advanced than previously thought. It also supports the view that Viking ships and seaborne activities were not as revolutionary as is commonly believed.   5 maps & 18 illustrations

UK £14·95 ISBN 1–898281–22–X approx. 245 x 170 mm/10" x 6½" 224 pages

A Guide to Late Anglo-Saxon England
From Alfred to Eadgar II   849-1074AD
Donald Henson

This guide has been prepared with the aim of providing the general readers with both an overview of the period and a wealth of background information. Facts and figures are presented in a way that makes this a useful reference handbook.

Contents include: The Origins of England; Physical Geography; Human Geography; English Society; Government and Politics; The Church; Language and Literature; Personal Names; Effects of the Norman Conquest. All of the kings from Alfred to Eadgar II are dealt with separately and there is a chronicle of events for each of their reigns. There are also maps, family trees and extensive appendices.

£12·95   ISBN 1–898281–21–1 245mm x 170mm/ 9½" x 6¾", 6 maps & 3 family trees 208 pp

Monasteriales Indicia
The Anglo-Saxon Monastic Sign Language

Edited with notes and translation by Debby Banham

The *Monasteriales Indicia* is one of very few texts which let us see how life was really lived in monasteries in the early Middle Ages. Written in Old English and preserved in a manuscript of the mid-eleventh century, it consists of 127 signs used by Anglo-Saxon monks during the times when the Benedictine Rule forbade them to speak. These indicate the foods the monks ate, the clothes they wore, and the books they used in church and chapter, as well as the tools they used in their daily life, and persons they might meet both in the monastery and outside. The text is printed here with a parallel translation. The introduction gives a summary of the background, both historical and textual, as well as a brief look at the later evidence for monastic sign language in England. Extensive notes provide the reader with details of textual relationships, explore problems of interpretation, and set out the historical implications of the text.

£6·95 A5 ISBN 0–9516209–4–0 96pp

Aspects of Anglo-Saxon Magic

Bill Griffiths

Magic is something special, something unauthorised; an alternative perhaps; even a deliberate cultivation of dark, evil powers. But for the Anglo-Saxon age, the neat division between mainstream and occult, rational and superstitious, Christian and pagan is not always easy to discern. To maintain its authority (or its monopoly?) the Church drew a formal line and outlawed a range of dubious practices (like divination, spells, folk healing) while at the same time conducting very similar rituals itself, and may even have adapted legends of elves to serve in a Christian explanation of disease as a battle between good and evil, between Church and demons; in other cases powerful ancestors came to serve as saints.

In pursuit of a better understanding of Anglo-Saxon magic, a wide range of topics and texts are examined in this book, challenging (constructively, it is hoped) our stereotyped images of the past and its beliefs.

Texts are printed in their original language (e.g. Old English, Icelandic, Latin) with New English translations. Contents include:– twenty charms; the English, Icelandic and Norwegian rune poems; texts on dreams, weather signs, unlucky days, the solar system; and much more.

£14·95. ISBN 1–898281–15–7   250mm x 175mm   10" x 7"   256pp

Anglo-Saxon Books

Frithgarth, Thetford Forest Park,
Hockwold-cum-Wilton, Norfolk IP26 4NQ
Tel: 01842 828430   Fax: 01842 828332
email: asbooks@englisc.demon.co.uk
A full list of our titles is available on our web site at
www.englisc.demon.co.uk or send us a s.a.e.

We accept payment by cheque, Visa, Eurocard and Mastercard.

UK deliveries add 10% up to a maximum of £2·50
Europe – including **Republic of Ireland** – add 10% plus £1 – all sent airmail
North America add 10% surface delivery, 30% airmail
Elsewhere add 10% surface delivery, 40% airmail
Overseas surface delivery 6 – 10 weeks; airmail 6 – 14 days

Most titles are available in North America from bookstores.